Sunshine And Shadow Or Stories From Crayford: For The Young Folk

William Henry Davenport Adams

SUNSHINE AND SHADOW:

OR,

STORIES FROM CRAYFORD.

FOR THE YOUNG FOLK.

BY

W. H. DAVENPORT ADAMS.

TALES FOR OUR YOUNG FOLK HERE ARE TOLD,
SIMPLE TALES AND TRUE—
OF ENGLISH LIFE, AND ENGLISH SCENES
WHICH HAPPY YEARS RENEW.
TALES OF HOPE, AND FAITH, AND LOVE,
OF YOUNG AMBITION'S DREAM,
OF CHILDHOOD'S PLEASURES AND ITS PAINS,—
THE BUBBLES ON LIFE'S STREAM!
TALES FOR OUR YOUNG FOLK, WHICH THE PEN
WILL NOT HAVE TRACED IN VAIN,
IF THEY WHO READ THEM ONCE SHOULD WISH
TO READ THEM O'ER AGAIN!

London:
SKEFFINGTON & SON, 163, PICCADILLY.
1888.

PREFACE.

THE writer hopes that the following Tales, which are all supposed to have a more or less direct connection with a quiet English provincial town, and are intended to shew how closely romance is associated with real life, will be found acceptable by young readers. They make no pretensions to a sensational character; but relate possible and probable incidents, such as are of frequent occurrence,—which might happen, with one or two exceptions, in the most ordinary lives,— and yet possess a distinctive interest; and they relate these incidents without affectation, in as simple a style as the writer could command. The seed gathered from various sources he has sown in English soil, and he trusts that the product will commend itself to English lads and lasses "in their teens." In old days it was always considered desirable that to stories for the young "a moral" should be tagged on in letters so large that no eye could fail to read them, in a form so conspicuous that the most graceless little reader could not overlook it! "We have changed all that;" and yet the writer thinks that there should be a purpose and an aim in everything one writes. He confesses that such a purpose will be found in each of his unpretending narratives; and it will be a satisfaction to him if his readers discover and apply it.

W. H. D. A.

CONTENTS.

———

I.

LOVE UNTO DEATH.

A STORY OF HARTMERE VILLA.

IN the whole town of Crayford—not a very extensive area. I admit, for Crayford is but a quiet "market-town and municipal borough" (as the Gazetteers say) in the far-off corner of a Midland county, and though it has everything decent and respectable about it, an old church and a county bank, a market-place and a police-station, it has no pretensions to populousness or extent, and makes very little noise in the world—in the whole town of Crayford, which, let me tell you, is as pretty and picturesque a place as one would wish to live in, struggling with easy indifference up hill and down dale, and surrounded by masses of foliage and by undulating hills, the boundaries of the valley of the Cray—in the whole town of Crayford you would not have found, some thirty years ago, a happier or more united couple than Mr. and Mrs. Hartmere, "the good Hartmeres" as everybody called them. Yet seldom were there two people more unlike.

Now, for my part, I have never believed that people of exactly the same temper, tastes, and character get on very well together. No; you want the effects of contrast and opposition; you want somebody "as *is* a somebody," and

A

not your own reflection. And this was the reason, I think, why Mr. and Mrs. Hartmere lived on such excellent terms; they were as unlike as husband and wife *ought* to be— even physically : for Mr. Hartmere was tall and angular ; Mrs. Hartmere short and rotund. And mentally : for Mr. Hartmere was a scholar, a philosopher, who knew more than everybody else had forgotten ; more than the parson and the attorney and the banker and the editor of our local paper taken in a lump (if I may be excused for placing four such distinguished persons in so undignified a juxtaposition) ; more, perhaps, than all the members of the Royal Society, to which, by the way, he belonged. He was, indeed, an ardent investigator of the sciences ; and no sooner did a new scientific treatise or review, in any of the European languages, appear, than it found its way to Hartmere Villa, where its gratified possessor made haste to find it a niche in one or other of his well-fitted bookcases.

Mr. Hartmere was not a scientific lecturer, nor a professor ; he loved knowledge for its own sake, and not for what might be made out of it. Having been successful in business in London, and acquired a small competency, he had returned to Crayford while yet in the prime of life, to devote himself to his favourite pursuits. Nor was he one of those votaries of science who hide their light under a bushel, and refuse to give up the illumination to their fellow-men : close-fisted misers, who spare their precious grains of learning as reluctantly as other misers part with their golden guineas.

No ; Mr. Hartmere was at the beck and call of anybody who wanted an explanation of a difficulty—a word of advice, the solution of some unexpected problem, such as often startles common-place men in the course of their daily work, and too often goes unsolved for want of a hint as to the right way of solving it. To the young men of Crayford, whose wits had been set in motion by the then novel system of competitive examinations, he was simply invaluable; infinitely better than Dictionary or Cyclopædia, because, by some mysterious law, Dictionaries and Cyclopædias seldom tell you the thing you most want to know. Nor are they so patient or so kind as was good Mr. Hartmere. And as Mr. Hartmere's purse was not less open than his mind and heart, you may fancy how great was his popularity among the young people of Crayford.

And this, mind you, was the only thing in which his wife resembled him. She was as popular as her husband. "That good, kind, amiable, generous, feeling-hearted, *dear* Mrs. Hartmere !"—and the speakers meant it, too. They were not mere words of conventional compliment, but came straight from the hearts of those who had benefitted by her liberality, been cheered and soothed by her sympathy, been guided or warned by her counsel. Not only the poor, but the well-to-do, joined in the chorus of praise, for she was always ready to lend her best silver tea-service, or her gilt spoons, or her handsomest epergne, or generously to supply any deficiency which perplexed the souls of the Crayford ladies when inclined towards hospitality, and genuine must be the Christianity of any housewife who will do such good deeds as these ! Moreover, she had an abundant store of the most wonderful receipts imaginable for all kinds of sweets and preserves, for rare soups and dainty puddings, for delicious liquors of home-concoction ; and these, too, were always at the disposal of her friends.

"Good, kind, dear Mrs. Hartmere !" So said the lads and lasses of Crayford when, several times in the winter, she threw open her best drawing-room for their entertainment, receiving them with a welcome so bright and sincere that it thawed them at once out of their usual conventional frigidity, and showing so ready a sympathy and so keen an enjoyment in *their* enjoyment, that nowhere else did the dance go so merrily, or the charade so successfully, as at Hartmere Villa! And then, when love-lone maidens or broken-hearted swains confided to her gentle ear their sad stories of true love that would not, or could not, run smooth, how charmingly she listened, as if she had never heard such a tale before!—and how prompt she was with practical and sensible advice!

"Dear, good, generous Mrs. Hartmere!" So, too, said the shopkeepers of Crayford, with whom she dealt in the frankest and most liberal spirit, never attempting to cheapen a really good article, and never keeping a tradesman waiting for the money he had fairly earned. And so said the poor, to whom she was as an angel from Heaven, so genial was her smile, so kind her speech, so active her interest, and so ready her assistance when she saw that it was deserved.

It is true that Mrs. Hartmere was as rotund of body as her husband was angular; as short as he was tall; as plump as he was meagre. It is true, too, that she was almost as ignorant as he was learned, and knew nothing of any science under heaven, except the science of making people happy, which is a science known only to a few rare spirits; but, as I have told you, she was as popular in Crayford as her husband, who, by general consent, had knowledge enough to serve both for his wife and himself and everybody else.

I am pleased to assure you that Mr. Hartmere never supposed his wife had any defect. His household was excellently

managed; there was plenty without extravagance, and order
without tyranny.   His "study" was all that a philosopher's
study ought to be : warm and snug in winter, fresh and airy in
summer ; everything in its place, and yet no sign of inter-
ference or meddling.   His books and papers were kept free
from dust, and yet were always where he wanted them.   Those
unfortunates who know what havoc is wrought when a busy
domestic is let loose in their favourite sanctum, to work her
wicked will among the sheets of the unfinished novel, or the
notes on the great speech at the meeting of the Society for the
Improvement of Dutch Ovens, or your correspondence on some
weighty subject with a certain eminent statesman, will appreciate
the good fortune of Mr. Hartmere!   And when he prepared to
sally forth on his daily constitutional, his hat and his gloves—
and his umbrella, if rain threatened, or great coat if the
thermometer had fallen,—were invariably ready to his hand.
When he sat down to dinner, he knew that the uplifted covers
would reveal his favourite dishes.   And, above all, he knew that
in his faithful wife he had that "dimidium animæ" of whom
the Latin poet speaks—that other half of his soul, who smiled
when he smiled, sorrowed—happily this was very seldom for
God had been merciful to them, because they were merciful to
others—when he sorrowed, rejoiced in his little scientific
triumphs, and shared to the full all his anticipations and realiza-
tions, all his disappointments, all his anxieties, and all his
pains, not less than all his pleasures.

   How, in such a wife, could he find anything wanting ?   True it
was, that her literary and scientific equipment was composed of a
morocco writing-case containing her private cash-book and her
household accounts, of the four rules of arithmetic, and some vague

ideas of syntax and geography—but what did that matter? From
the elevated view-point of his devoted affection, his wife seemed
to him not less well-informed or accomplished than Mrs.
Layland, the banker's wife, the acknowledged *belle esprit* or
blue stocking of Crayford, who read " The Contemporary "
and " The Journal of Mind and Matter," spoke French (which
no Frenchman understood), wrote verses (which nobody could
scan), and was prepared to start off full gallop in a discussion
upon all things, human and divine, at a moment's notice,—
who, moreover, most thoroughly bored him as his wife never
did! He never spoke to her of his scientific researches; but
often, at eventide, when they were alone, and she sat opposite
to him at his study-table, manipulating with swift fingers one of
those masterpieces of embroidery which were the admiration
and despair of the ladies of Crayford, he would take up some
book by a true and noble writer, and read aloud its choicest
passages, while she, as he read, would grow more and more
excited, until, dropping her knitting-needles in order to wipe
away a tear or two, she would exclaim,—" How fine that is!
How noble!" That was all; and for her husband it was
quite enough. He left her to her thoughts, which she wanted
words to express, though Mr. Hartmere could read them easily
with his tender and experienced eyes.

For mortals, however, even the brightest sky is never without
a cloud, and on that of the Hartmeres a single shadow rested—
they had no children. They had long become reconciled to
this misfortune, though to them, with their infinite capacity of
loving, it was a very great misfortune; and found some com-
pensation in the pleasure they took in each other's society. I
have often observed this to be the case with childless couples;

husband and wife clinging to one another all the more closely where there are no children, to share their affection and divide their attention ; for though, in one sense, children form an additional bond of union, yet, on the other hand, they create separate interests, which not infrequently raise between husband and wife an invisible, perhaps, but not an unreal barrier.

As for the Hartmeres, apart from their mutual attachment, they had the daily occupations which filled up every moment, and allowed them little leisure to feel that anything was wanting. Mr. Hartmere, had, of course, his scientific pursuits, his correspondence, his young neophytes ; while, as for his wife, her avocations were as numerous as they were various. There were her pensioners, her poor people, the sick and distressed, to be visited ; there were kindly relations to be maintained with old friends, whose children she had seen grow up into men and women ; there was her household to be controlled and directed, so that all its movements should be as smooth and easy as those of an automatic machine ; there were her servants to be taught and trained, and in due time married advantageously, and settled in little homes of their own, where her wise lessons brought forth good fruit for many a year.

Then she was incomparably skilful with her needle, and it was her ingenious hand, guided by a fine natural taste, which had covered with graceful embroidery Mr. Hartmere's dressing-gown, the couch on which he sometimes indulged in a brief siesta, the footstool on which he rested his feet, the curtains which drooped in flowing folds over his library-windows. And as her hand was not less liberal than it was skilful, scarcely an infant came into the little world of Crayford—at least, among her friends—but immediately upon its arrival a

messenger appeared from Mrs. Hartmere laden with a supply
of caps and robes and other articles, each of which was a
marvel of exquisite handiwork.

You will not wonder then that the first name which fell upon
the ear of any visitor to Crayford was that of Hartmere—of
Mr. Hartmere who had founded *this*, and Mrs. Hartmere who
had contributed to *that*, of Mr. Hartmere, the great scholar,
who knew everything, and Mrs. Hartmere, the soul of charity,
who helped everything. To Mr. Beecham, the rich stock-
broker, who had bought a house and grounds in the immediate
neighbourhood of Crayford, with the view of residing there
permanently, the name of Hartmere became perfectly dis-
tasteful, as any visitor who called upon him did not fail to
mention it half-a-dozen times at least in the course of conversation. Mr. Beecham soon made himself acquainted with the
history of this charming old couple, but the dislike which
their popularity had from the first engendered in his vain and
pretentious nature grew into positive antipathy when he
discovered that Mr. Hartmere possessed a library which far
surpassed his own in extent and value. For Mr. Beecham was
a collector—a collector of books, not a reader, for he seldom
opened any of his thousands of volumes. Book-collecting was
his hobby, and he loved to decorate his purchases with the
most resplendent of bindings, and then, as they shone upon the
shelves of his book-cases in gold and colours, like a regiment
of gorgeously equipped troops, marshalled in the strictest
array—rows of morocco in one shelf, rows of calf in another—
he would stand and enjoy their appearance, and point them out
to his guests with as much pride and complacency as if he had
mastered their contents, instead of being utterly ignorant of them.

There was nothing in Mr. Beecham himself, as he very well knew, to command respect or awaken the admiration and applause which were to him as the breath of his nostrils ; and you may conceive his mortification, therefore, when he found that in the one thing which he relied upon to excite the astonishment of Crayford society, he was inferior after all to " that confounded Hartmere, whom everybody talked about so disgustingly ! " It was true that Mr. Hartmere's library made nothing of the show that Mr. Beecham's did. Mr. Hartmere's moderate competency did not allow him to spend hundreds of pounds on the outside of his books, but his library had been carefully collected, and presented a noble array of the master-pieces of literature, ancient and modern, English and foreign. Mr. Beecham had sense enough to know that in intrinsic value his own could not come any way near it, and that even from a pecuniary point of view it was vastly inferior. Worthless books do not sell well, though their bindings may be of the costliest description. Whereas Mr. Hartmere admitted to his shelves none which had not some merit of their own, while he had collected many new and precious editions of the early writers, Elzevirs and the like, specimens of Caxton and Baskerville, which the bibliophile stared at with a hungry and covetous eye.

That library of Mr. Hartmere's became Mr. Beecham's *bite noire.* He thought of it by day, and he dreamed of it by night. If he could but add it to his own, he saw himself the proud owner of a library such as few men in England could hope to match. Was this possible ? He was a younger man by fifteen years than Mr. Hartmere ; in all probability he would survive him, and he would then—but to pursue this train of thought made him giddy with delighted anticipation, until the dread reflection sobered him that life was uncertain, and that, after all, Mr. Hartmere, apparently a healthy man, might outlive *him !* Besides, he might bequeath it to some public institution, or order it by his will to be sold by public auction, when the different lots would undoubtedly command prices beyond even Mr. Beecham's present means. This latter result seemed so feasible, nay, so certain, as Mr. Beecham dwelt upon it, that he resolved to cut down his expenditure, and adopt every expedient of increasing his fortune, that he might eventually be in a position to bid against all competitors for the coveted prize. His hopes were greatly stimulated when, a few months after he had come to this determination, and surprised society by reducing his establishment and dropping his dinner-parties, a liberal legacy was left to him by a wealthy uncle—on the principle, I suppose, that to him who hath more shall be given. Looking about for a profitable investment for this windfall, he was on the point of investing it in the old county bank, when he unexpectedly obtained secret, but trustworthy, information that it was in a dangerously insecure condition, and took care to find another channel for his money. It then occurred to him that most of Mr. Hartmere's savings, so he had heard, were deposited in this bank, which had long borne a very high character, and enjoyed the confidence of the principal gentry of the county. Further inquiries revealed to him the fact that in a few days the bank must inevitably come down with a crash ; that the partners had wasted, not only their own capital, but their depositors' moneys, in wild speculations ; and the reflection was borne in upon his mind that he ought at once to convey this information privately to Mr. Hartmere, and enable him to withdraw his capital, or so much as he could save of it, while there was yet time. He sat down to his desk to write, when the tempter whispered in his ear, "If Mr. Hartmere should be ruined he will have to sell his library, and you can step in before anybody else and offer him a good price for it. He will then be nearly as well off as he is now, and will not even lose the enjoyment of his beloved books, for they will of course be as much at his disposal under your roof as they are under his own. But they will be *yours*—yes, *yours!* And the Beecham Library will be the glory of the Midlands! And as the Beecham Library it will go down to posterity, so that in years to come men shall say, 'Have you seen the great library collected by the celebrated Mr. Beecham?'" All this was very mean and pitiful; but greed had taken possession of the man's soul, and so he did not write.

The bank put up its shutters, and Mr. Hartmere was ruined ! You can imagine the wretchedness, the anxiety, the heavy trouble which an event so unexpected and so disastrous caused in Crayford, and how deeply it was felt at Hartmere Villa. Yet there, at least, the blow was lightened by the great affection which prevailed between husband and wife—an affection which was proof against every human ill. As soon as decency permitted, Mr. Beecham made his appearance, had a private interview with Mr. Hartmere, and with all the ingenuity at his command, proposed to purchase the library, offering a price which would secure his friends, as he called them, against any privation or change in their mode of living.

Much surprised and not a little wounded, Mr. Hartmere said he would consult his wife before giving a definite reply. For himself, he would prefer a dry crust in the midst of his beloved books to the most sumptuous repast surrounded by empty shelves. But then his wife! Yes, she must be thought of!— ought she to suffer the pangs of poverty, when it was in his power to ward them off from her? Ah, he had not fathomed the depths of his wife's devoted love! Even he was ignorant of all that her unselfishness, her tender spirit of self-sacrifice could achieve and endure. Had she known how to put her feelings into verse, she would probably have addressed her husband in language something like that of a poet of our own times—

    " Our love is not a fading, earthly flower :—
      Its wingèd seed dropped down from Paradise,
      And, nursed by day and night, by sun and shower,
      Doth momently to fresher beauty rise :
      To us the leafless autumn is not bare,
      Nor winter's rattling boughs lack lusty green.
      Our summer hearts make summer's fulness, where
      No leaf, or bud, or blossom may be seen."

Yes, though a "leafless autumn" had come upon them, the "fresher beauty" and deeper tenderness of his wife's affection filled it with "a summer's fulness." He had scarcely broached Mr. Beecham's proposal before she brushed it aside indignantly. "What! sell your library? your books? the books you have treasured so fondly, of which you have made such noble use? Never, never, husband! Why do you think of doing a thing so dreadful?" Was he afraid of poverty? she said. Well, but they would not be poor, or, at least, not very poor. Of course, he understood nothing of book-keeping, or he would know upon how small a sum two old people could live comfortably. What was left of his savings would be quite sufficient. They would have to give up their charities and hospitalities, it is true—and he, poor fellow! would be unable to buy any more books. They would let furnished a couple of rooms to eke out their income, and dispense with a servant—servants were so wasteful !—and having paid all their creditors, he would still be able to retain— his library !

So it came to pass that Mr. Hartmere declined the offer made by Mr. Beecham, whose mind was much disturbed by conflicting emotions : by disappointment at the failure of his cherished project, and remorse at the ruin of his friend, which, he was conscious, a word from him might have averted.   He felt that he had been guilty of a great sin, and to no purpose ; and, believe me, there is no pang so keen as that of the sinner whose sin has failed to prosper.   When Tallyrand said that a blunder was worse than a crime, he knew that an unprofitable crime was the greatest of all blunders.   So Mr. Beecham was wroth with himself when his treachery had proved un- successful.

It was not in Mr. Hartmere's nature to leave to his wife the sole burden of supporting their diminished household.   He was not young enough or energetic enough to resume a commercial career, even if he had had the necessary capital ; but he con- ceived the idea of turning to account his scientific acquirements, and announced to all whom it might concern that he was prepared to give instruction, in schools or privately, in the various branches of Science he had so assiduously cultivated. As his reputation had spread far beyond the little world of Crayford, he speedily found himself provided with as much work of this kind as he could undertake.   Young men of good family, in training for the University, were only too glad to be "coached" in mathematics and similar subjects by so competent a teacher ; and the liberal fees he received swelled by degrees into an income which rendered unnecessary the rigid economy on which Mrs. Hartmere had resolved.

The world went very well then with this tender-hearted couple —went very well for some happy and uneventful months. But in time the different mode of life began to tell upon Mr. Hartmere. After men reach a certain age it is always very difficult for them to adapt themselves to fresh conditions and take up novel habits. It was evident to observant eyes that Mr. Hartmere aged rapidly,—and that his constitution, never very robust, was yielding under a strain and pressure it had never before been called upon to bear. Within two years from the failure of the Bank he passed away. On the agonizing grief of his poor wife I need not dwell; but it may be said of him with truth, what is too often said as an empty formality, that he died deeply respected and universally lamented.

Mr. Beecham felt a fresh thrill of compunction when the funeral procession of the dead scholar passed his house, but the feeling soon gave way to pleasurable anticipation. At last he would be able to gratify his desire, to realize the dream that had so long absorbed him. He *had* outlived Mr. Hartmere, and no doubt the coveted library would soon become his. He began to revel in roseate visions of coming celebrity, and with his mind's eye saw long vistas of pilgrims coming from all parts of England and Scotland, the United States, and Australia, from all countries where the English tongue was spoken, to admire the great Beecham library.

He waited impatiently for the time when, without violating any social conventionality, he might call upon the widow, and renew his offer of purchase, yet when it at length arrived he was almost ill with excitement. No ardent lover, intent on hearing from the lips of the woman he loved, the "yes" or "no" which will decide his happiness or ensure his misery, could have experienced a deeper anxiety. His knees knocked against each other, and his hands trembled, as he waited admission at the door of Hartmere Villa, and his voice positively faltered as he asked the servant whether her mistress could receive him.

He was shown at once into the library, and, but for the pale face, sad eyes, and mourning attire of the afflicted widow, might have supposed that nothing had occurred since he visited it. The books were in their usual order; the table, loaded with writing implements, was in its accustomed place by the French windows, which opened on the well-kept garden; the scholar's silver inkstand was full, and the pens were ranged by the side of the well-known desk, on which lay the manuscript he was working at when stricken by his fatal illness. His easy chair stood in its old position, with the footstool embroidered by Mrs. Hartmere's laborious fingers; and she, too, was there, where she had sat evening after evening for so many happy years, plying the needle as was her wont, though no longer, it is true, as a pastime, but as a stern necessity, to provide her with the means of livelihood; for Mr. Hartmere's death-bed had, of course, deprived her of almost all her income, and to maintain herself it was indispensable that she should work, and work assiduously. It was upon this sad circumstance, indeed, that Mr. Beecham chiefly built his hopes of success.

He entered upon his subject, nevertheless, with a good deal of embarrassment. Mrs. Hartmere, we need hardly say, had no idea of the real object of his visit, but regarding it as one of sympathy, expressed her thanks with evident sincerity.

"I am truly pleased to see you," she exclaimed; "my dear husband esteemed you so highly. Since you fixed your residence here he seemed to grow young again; he so enjoyed conversing with you about his books. I quite easily understood it. A man so learned as he was naturally liked to talk with other men of learning, for I was unable to discuss with him on the subjects he loved best. Often and often in my heart I have felt deeply grateful to you for the pleasure you have given him. It was you, too, who taught me my ignorance; hearing you talk together, I learned how much he had previously missed in me which he found in you, for he was so good, so noble, that he had never allowed me to become aware of my deficiencies; but now that he has gone, and there is no longer any attraction for you in this house, I am still grateful to you for coming to speak to me of him whom we both loved."

Mr. Beecham felt an odd sensation in the throat while Mrs. Hartmere spoke her innocent utterances, and it was with some difficulty that he at last approached the object of his visit. Mrs. Hartmere, as soon as she comprehended it, turned pale—then crimson—tears gathered in her eyes, and in a voice choked with emotion, she exclaimed—

"Sell the library! Sell *his* library!—the library which he collected with such pains and patience! Impossible! My dear Mr. Beecham, it is my only consolation, my single source of comfort! Every book on yonder shelves is associated with him, and so long as they are around me I do not feel as if he and I were entirely separated. You see, I keep them in as good order as if their owner were to return to-morrow. It is here I sit at my work, for nowhere else can I think of him with so much satisfaction and recall the beautiful things which he read to me in the evenings."

"But the sum of money I am willing to offer," interrupted Mr. Beecham, "would prove of solid value to you. It would keep you all the rest of your days in comfort."

"My dear sir, I need very little money, I assure you! I live on so little, and my wants are so few. The proceeds of my work, with the remnant of my husband's fortune, will support me without difficulty."

"But if you were taken ill——."

"God would raise up some friend to assist me! For this I know, that I will *never* sell my husband's library."

Mr. Beecham urged every argument he could think of, but the only answer he could get was—"I will *never, never* sell his library!" At length his insistance ruffled the good temper of the widow, who started from her chair, and with outstretched finger motioned him to the door. "Not another word, sir," she exclaimed; "would you insult your friend's widow under her own roof? Never think of it, never speak of it again. So long as I live I will not part with my husband's treasured companions. Good morning, Mr. Beecham."

There was something heroic in this constancy, for Mrs. Hartmere's means were now so limited that it was only by the most rigid economy she made them suffice. The proceeds of her skilful needle were necessarily scanty; there was not always a demand for her kind of fancy work, and it was very poorly paid. The friends who patronised her at first were soon supplied, and she could find a market only at the shops. As Crayford boasted of but one establishment for the sale of embroidery, she was compelled to send her goods to London, where the

B

competition was very keen, and prices were exceedingly low. Mrs. Hartmere's life, therefore, in these days, was an arduous struggle, though she preserved her old expression of content-ment, and regretted only that she could no longer gratify the impulses of her charitable heart.

It is true that, without disposing of the precious library, she might have realized a considerable addition to her pittance by the sale of her house, which was large and handsomely built, in good condition, and surrounded by a beautiful garden. But she clung to the house almost as closely as to the library. It was associated with all that was brightest and dearest in her past; it had been the cherished home of her husband's happiest years; and to have parted with it would have seemed to her like parting with him for a second time. Those inanimate, voiceless stones! how in the course of years we come to love them, and how eloquent they grow in their silent witness to the joys and sorrows, pleasures and pains, of the days we have left behind us!

So Mrs. Hartmere was deaf to all the recommendations and entreaties of her lawyer and her friends; and having been left perfectly untrammelled by her husband's will, which placed everything at her sole disposal, she continued to live on in her big empty mansion, enduring many privations, and gradually forsaken by those who had loaded her with smiles and flatteries in the time of her prosperity. For Society altogether failed to understand her passionate devotion to the past, and began to shrug its shoulders, and turn aside from her as from a miser or a lunatic. Perhaps, however, there was more of pity than censure in its comments—the aggravating pity which superior wisdom bestows upon inferior ignorance:—

"That poor Mrs. Hartmere!" said Mrs. Grundy; "how surprisingly her husband's death has changed her! She is not at all like her old self; but then you know, my dear, that with all her excellent qualities—and nobody will deny that she had many, oh, many charmingly good qualities—she had never *a very strong head!*"

So the Mrs. Grundys of the world compassionated her very much, but they forgot to visit her; and, to speak the truth, the few who *did* call had reason to complain of their cold reception. Sorrow had rendered Mrs. Hartmere suspicious; and she was ever on her guard lest her visitors should give her the advice she did not want instead of the sympathy she coveted. She was afraid that each fresh intruder would repeat the stereotyped formula—"Why do you not part with your house, my dear Mrs. Hartmere? So much too large for you, you know! And so very expensive, is it not? Oh! *not* expensive? Well, you know best,—but a nice little cottage now I should have thought would have been *so* much—oh, so *very* much better, you know!" And so on—and so on—until sometimes the poor widow's irritated and over-strained nerves gave way, and when her unconscious persecutor turned her back, she would throw herself into her husband's empty chair, and relieve herself by a passion of tears.

At length she recurred to her old idea of letting lodgings, the usual refuge of broken-down respectability, and in one of the front windows of Hartmere Villa might be seen a printed announcement of "Furnished Apartments to Let." There it remained, I am sorry to say, for days and days, and weeks and weeks, until every boy and girl in Crayford was familiar with it, and regarded it as one of the institutions of the place, like the

old pump, and the pound, and the fire-engine station. Crayford was not frequented as a summer resort, and the stranger
who visited it for business purposes, or the artist who came to
sketch in its picturesque neighbourhood, or the angler to fish
in the bright little river that meandered through its fields,
usually took up his quarters at the comfortable hotel in its
principal street, or at one of its cozy little inns. Then, again,
Hartmere Villa was situated quite at the other end of the town,
away from the railway, in a locality which was very pretty and
secluded, and though this seclusion had been the special
attraction which recommended it to the retiring and retired
votary of science, it was not likely to prove so inviting to
ordinary and common-place minds.

One day, however, a young man, a very young man, whose
upper lip as yet was shaded by only a thin line of silken
down, after wandering through all the streets of Crayford, and
examining (from the outside) the few houses which were
prepared to take in the stranger and do for him, struck into
the Winsham Road, and in due course found himself in front
of Hartmere Villa. "What a delightful retreat !" he muttered,
" what glorious elms and noble chestnuts ! and I can just catch
a peep of a pretty garden ; but is the place inhabited ? There
seems a strange air of neglect about it. What's this ? ' Furnished Apartments to Let !' How curious ! Apartments to let
in a house of this kind ! Quite a first-class villa ! Well, at all
events," and he sighed heavily, " they will be far above my
figure, or I should hugely like to settle down in such an
Arcadian nook !" He turned away, and walked a few steps ;
hesitated, halted, turned again towards the house, and exclaiming, " Hang it all, there can be no harm in asking," seized the

handle of the door-bell, and rang a peal which resounded through the empty house like a charge of artillery. "Confound it," said the youth, "who would have thought that an old door-bell would have made such a tintinnabulation!"

. In a minute or two the door was cautiously opened, and a lady, advanced in years, presented herself. It would be difficult to say who felt the more nervous—the blushing young man, or the unaccustomed lodging-house keeper; but after a few stammered sentences, Mrs. Hartmere came to understand that the stranger wanted to rent a bedroom and sitting-room, and the stranger found that her charges were so unexpectedly moderate as to fall within the range of his attenuated purse. If Mrs. Hartmere had had any experience of her calling, she would, of course, have demanded a reference, or "a week's rent in advance," but she was prepossessed by the young stranger's modest appearance and courteous air, and in a few minutes the bargain was completed. The lodger returned to the railway station for his belongings, which were all comprised in one small portmanteau, and, before evening, was comfortably domiciled in Hartmere Villa.

"A man in the house" is recognized by most housekeepers as a disturbing element—a "factor" which completely alters the character of "the situation," and accounts for everything that goes wrong, from a thunderstorm to a crash among the crockery. But Mrs. Hartmere made no change in the habits that had crystallized about her since her husband's death. From the address on the letters which he occasionally received she had learned his name (she had actually forgotten to ask it!), and as it was Scotch—Alexander Maclean—she was a little surprised to find that he spoke English with the purest possible accent.

Mr. Alexander Maclean was a model lodger! He made no noise in the house, exacted no attendance, went out at the same hour every morning, and returned at the same hour every evening, and after a frugal meal of milk and bread and butter, or porridge and a biscuit, sat down to his studies, whatever they might be, with evident zest, pursuing them far into the night with the aid of the tiny oil-lamp, which was all the illumination he allowed himself. Mrs. Hartmere gradually discovered that he had more books than clothes, and that the books were old and worn, very unlike the splendid volumes which glittered on Mr. Beecham's shelves! She observed, too, that he seemed to grow paler and thinner every week, and she wondered whether he ever dined, and where, since his fare at home was too meagre (as she said to herself) "to keep a fly alive." Even on Sundays he went out for his dinner; to save his kind landlady trouble, he remarked, though she protested that it would be a pleasure rather than a trouble to prepare for him some dainty little dish. There could be no doubt about his poverty, though he paid his rent every Saturday with exemplary punctuality, throwing down the few coins with quite a lordly air, as if he were the master of thousands. He had all the proud reserve of his countrymen, who are slower at taking their neighbours into their confidence than any other people in the world.

It was impossible but that in Mrs. Hartmere's kindly nature a deep interest should soon be developed in this quiet, self-controlled young man, who was so nervously anxious to avoid giving her trouble, and thanked her with almost painful emphasis for every trivial service she rendered him. And he, too, could not but feel some concern for the silent woman, who had evidently seen better days, and now lived a life of seclusion and self-denial in her handsome mansion.

Each saw that the other had a story, and each waited for the other to break the ice. At first, when Maclean discovered that the proprietress of Hartmere Villa lived entirely alone, did all her own domestic work, and was content with as spare a dietary as he himself was obliged to live upon, he set her down in his own mind as a wretched miser. But he changed his opinion when, one day, he saw her giving a bottle of wine to a poor woman for her sick husband. She who gave her wine to the poor while she herself drank water could not be a miser. After this, partly from natural goodness of heart, and partly from a wish to make amends for the injustice he had done her in his thoughts, he sought every opportunity of rendering assistance. He executed her little commissions in the town; he carried upstairs or down any articles that taxed her failing strength; and often entered into cordial conversation with her, instead of restricting his remarks to a few frigid and conventional phrases. Ultimately they came to be on the friendliest terms, and, one day, Maclean, was actually led to unburden himself to his kindly landlady.

On that day he had returned home, looking so worn and wan, that Mrs. Hartmere was quite alarmed, and showed so kind and delicate a sympathy that the young man's reserve gave way. He confessed that he felt very ill; his head was dizzy, he suffered from internal pains, and had no appetite for food. Mrs. Hartmere made him lie down on the sofa, wrapped him up, and in a few minutes brought him a glass of one of those marvellous cordials in the confection of which she had of old displayed such skill; and when he had somewhat recovered,

informed him, in her motherly way, that he must not go to bed
"on an empty stomach," and invited him to dine with her.

Maclean's physical weakness had undermined his pride. He
was hungry, nay, almost famished—and the invitation was
pressed upon him with so much delicacy and cordiality that he
could not refuse it. Accordingly he dined with Mrs. Hartmere,
sitting in the very place which her husband had formerly occupied for so many years ; and if she could not repress a pang at
the unusual sight she dissembled her emotion, and smiled
benignantly on her pallid guest. I need hardly say that, on
this occasion, she had departed from her usual abstemiousness,
and both she and Maclean enjoyed a hearty dinner—a luxury
which neither of them had known for a considerable period.
Afterwards they fell into a confidential conversation, so that when
they parted for the night Mrs. Hartmere warmly pressed the
young man's hand, and said with much emotion, " Good night,
my dear child, good night ! "

Alexander Maclean was nineteen years old, and had been an
orphan since he was ten. An uncle had been at the charge of
his education, and had intended him to complete his course of
study at the University of Edinburgh ; but his death had
unexpectedly thrown the young man on his own resources, and
after much advertizing and correspondence, he had been
engaged as a clerk in the great Crayford factory on the other
side of the town. He had a younger sister living, towards
whose support he contributed weekly, and he was also trying to
put aside out of his small salary a sufficient sum of money to
enable him to return to Edinburgh and take his degree, which
he seemed to think was the "open sesame" that would admit
him to fame and competency. His salary was 30s. a week, and

it was evident to Mrs. Hartmere that with these deductions, it must be inadequate to provide for his daily needs. His illness was due to insufficient sustenance, and the good lady made up her mind that such a state of things should no longer exist.

Next day, summoning up all her courage, she invited him to board with her for a small addition to his weekly rent. "It will cost you no more than you are paying now," she said, "and you will have wholesome food, while it will be no more trouble to me to cook for two persons than for one. Besides, in my old age, I often feel dull and melancholy, and your company will be a pleasure which I shall truly appreciate." Maclean at first fell back on his stiff Scotch reserve, but Mrs. Hartmere would not be denied, and the matter was ultimately settled to her entire satisfaction.

From that day Mrs. Hartmere renewed her interest in life. She enjoyed her frequent conversations with her protegé, and listened with unfailing interest to his anecdotes of his early years, and his descriptions of the romantic and sublime scenery of "bonny Scotland." She encouraged him to speak of the sister he loved so well, of his hopes and his projects for the future, and sympathized with the brave young fellow's resolution to prosecute his scientific researches and gain a reputation as a *savant*. He made light, for youth is always sanguine, of the obstacles in his path, though he did not conceal the difficulty he experienced from want of books. For books of the high class and standard reputation which he urgently required were usually very dear, and he could not afford to purchase them, while circulating libraries naturally ignore them because they would find no favour with the readers of light literature, who are their principal patrons.

One day, when he had dwelt with even more than his accustomed earnestness on this urgent need of his, Mrs. Hartmere fell into a brown study. This industrious and patient young student reminded her of her husband, who had often spoken of the troubles and trials of his early manhood. " If he were living now," she said to herself, " how he would have loved this young man ! With what pleasure he would have assisted him in his studies, and by his explanations have smoothed the path which he now finds so laborious ! My dear husband ! How many there are whom he taught to get their living, and owe to his generous instructions the very bread which they eat ! He was so good, so liberal ! He kept nothing to himself, not even his learning ; it was a luxury to him to share it with others. What a pity it is for poor Maclean that I cannot replace Mr. Hartmere."

These reflections led to others. " He is in want of books, this poor Alick—he cannot afford to buy, and is unable to borrow them. Suppose that he should be in need of some now in this house ? Hartmere used to say that he had collected all the best authorities—then, possibly, Alick would find amongst them . . ." But here, at first, she halted. She could not all at once reconcile herself to the idea of a stranger handling her beloved husband's books. The generous thought took root in her mind, however, and speedily matured. A good deed, she reflected, could never be done too soon ; and so, one fine day, Maclean, to his unbounded astonishment, was ushered into the noble room which contained Mr. Hartmere's library.

He gazed around him with the rapture a lover of books and a student would naturally feel at such a sight. He went from bookcase to bookcase ; he repeated aloud the well-known titles of

famous works which embodied the wisdom and experience of the
master-spirits of all ages and all countries, for not a single department of literature was unrepresented there. It was, however,
in scientific authorities that Mr. Hartmere's collection was
specially rich, and to these Maclean eagerly turned his attention.

"Oh, Mrs. Hartmere, what treasures you have here!"

"Yes, is it not so?" she replied, with a tear in her eyes, but
a smile on her lips. "Treasures they are, indeed, and my
poor husband loved them dearly—so dearly that I have never
been able to make up my mind to part with them, though they
would realize, I am told, a sum which would enable me to live in
affluence for the remainder of my life. But both this library and
this house are consecrated to my husband's memory; and never
will I allow them, while I live, to pass into a stranger's hands.
I am sure, however, that he would be only too pleased, were he
alive, to assist a young man like you; and therefore, Alick,
from this time forward they are at your disposal. Read them
as you will and when you will; but take care of them, for in
my eyes they are sacred."

I shall not attempt to describe Maclean's gratitude. His
greatest difficulty was swept away; the Hartmere library contained the very books he had yearned for, and night after
night he gave himself up to their perusal, with a feeling that he
was now on the road to Fame. At first he took to his own room
the authorities he wished to study, one volume at a time; but
as he often found it necessary to consult several simultaneously,
he was invited to spend his evenings in the library, where Mrs.
Hartmere became his constant companion, knitting industriously
while he read or wrote. He was not allowed, however, to
occupy the chair which had belonged to her husband, and a

separate table was brought in for his accommodation, that Mr. Hartmere's might be left untouched, with the spectacles still lying on the open manuscript.

Yet Maclean did not feel wholly at ease. He often asked himself how it was that Mrs. Hartmere managed to supply the daily meals for both of them on a pittance very little more than had previously furnished her own. He feared that she drew upon her own resources, which he knew were very limited, and, therefore, he grew anxious to find out some means of adding to his income, that he might pay a larger sum for his board and lodging, while continuing his weekly remittances to his sister. But no opportunity at first presented itself. Maclean and Mrs. Hartmere by this time were close friends, and much of the young Scotchman's reserve thawed away in the sunshine of the domestic happiness which Mrs. Hartmere's genial affection secured him. He gave to her his fullest confidences. In the course of his evening studies, when he came upon some passage of exceptional beauty, he would sometimes exclaim, "Oh, this is splendid, ma'am! shall I read it to you?"

And he would read with just emphasis, and due expression, the passage which had pleased him.

On the first occasion of his doing so he was surprised at her silence when he had finished reading; and raising his eyes towards the widow to see whether she had been impressed by it, he observed that she was sitting motionless, with her hands clasped upon her knees, and the tears rolling down her furrowed cheeks.

"My dear lady," he exclaimed, "what have I done? Have I pained you?"

She wiped away the tell-tale drops, resumed her knitting, and replied in a tremulous voice,

"No, no, on the contrary, I was delighted. But, all of a sudden, I recollected the passage as one which my husband was very fond of, and had read to me more than once. Your tastes, I see, are just the same; you will be exactly like him when you are older, I am sure of it! Now, when you come upon anything in a book which particularly pleases you, read it to me, as you have done this evening, and perhaps I shall again be fortunate enough to recall it to memory."

Thenceforth Maclean exercised all his ingenuity in endeavouring to hit upon the books her husband had generally read, and the passages he had selected for reading aloud. This was by no means an idle experiment. It can never be lost time or lost labour to seek after what is fine, and true, and beautiful, and nothing but good can come of the search. So that even after his death the old man was faithful to his self-imposed task of instructing young minds, and guiding them in the path of true intellectual culture.

So the weeks slipped by. Maclean was surrounded by comforts and affectionate attentions to which he had long been a stranger; and yet a shade of care and anxiety rested on his expressive countenance. His good friend, who watched over him as tenderly as if he had been her son, was disturbed by this change of aspect; but to her cautious questions, she could get no other answer then that nothing ailed him—nothing was the matter—and remembering his Scotch blood, she was afraid to push her inquiries too closely. But, one evening, when she had been reading the newspapers, she made a remark on the depression of trade which drew from him a deep sigh, and he suddenly broke out—

"Mother, why should I keep anything from you who are so

good and kind. to me? Besides, you must soon know it."

"Know what, Alick?" she interrupted with a little cry of alarm, fearing, for the moment, that he was about to confess to some misconduct which could no longer be hidden.

"Well, mother"—for by this tender name he was accustomed to call Mrs. Hartmere—"our firm have for some months been trading at a loss, in the hope that things would improve; but as no such good fortune seems possible, they have determined at length on making great reductions in their staff, and I am sadly afraid that the office I hold is one of those which will be done away with."

"Well, Alick?"

"Well, no, ill, mother, *very* ill—for then I must go out into the world again, and forfeit, at all events for a time—my hope of completing my University career. And, besides, my dear sister Janet. God knows what will become of *her* when I am discharged penniless into the streets of Crayford."

"You will not go into the streets of Crayford; you will remain here with your second mother, until some opening for your talents and industry can be found; and you will send for your sister to live with us, Alick. There is plenty of room in Hartmere Villa, and I dare to say that our Heavenly Father will not let us starve."

"Oh, mother, you are too good—too unselfish—too noble! How can I ever repay you? Words of gratitude sound so chill and formal. I want to *do* something which will show you that I am grateful in my heart of hearts!"

Next day, to Mrs. Hartmere's intense surprise, a visitor made his appearance at the Villa. He proved to be an old friend of her late husband, and, like him, a scientist, and the two investigators had formerly carried on a very active correspond-ence. He had been travelling in the Southern counties, and was unwilling to pass through Crayford without paying his respects to his friend's widow. He was desirous of ascertaining also whether Mr. Hartmere had left among his papers any notes upon a question which greatly interested him.

Mrs. Hartmere showed him into the library, where, after a short search, Professor Huxtable found what he was in search of on young Maclean's table.

"Ah," he cried, "I see that I have been anticipated, and that some person is engaged on the very same problem. I suppose the writings on this table were the work of one of your husband's pupils, and that his notes got mixed up with them?"

Mrs. Hartmere immediately launched out into a narrative of Alick Maclean's experiences, and with honest eloquence dwelt on his fine qualities, his noble conduct, and his great talents.

"How old is this wonder of yours?" enquired the Professor, smiling.

"He is just twenty."

"Only twenty!" exclaimed the Professor, with surprise; "only twenty, and so well-informed, and far advanced in the abstrusest mathematics! I should like such a young man for my Secretary, for I am getting old and need skilled assistance in the calculations I have in hand. Unfortunately, I am not rich, and could give only a very moderate salary, but the situation might be advantageous, as he would have numerous opportunities of prosecuting his researches; and, at the same time, of making himself known. I should not want all his time, and would make it my business to help him on in the world. You must introduce me to him; I will call again."

But as he spoke the door opened, and in rushed Maclean, pale and agitated.

"Well, Alick?" cried Mrs. Hartmere, advancing towards him.

"The blow has fallen; the works are shut up; and we are all dismissed, with a fortnight's salary in lieu of notice."

"So much the better!" exclaimed Mrs. Hartmere, with a smile.

"So much the better, mother?—But oh, I see you have a visitor; pray excuse my rudeness, my want of consideration."

"Let me introduce you to Professor Huxtable, who is anxious to make your acquaintance."

"Professor Huxtable! I count this a very great honour, sir," said Maclean, accepting the Professor's offered hand, "ever since I studied your valuable works I have longed to know you."

"Mrs. Hartmere," said the Professor, kindly, after a few commonplace observations had been exchanged, "has explained to me your anxieties; and I hope, and think, I can relieve them. I want to engage the services of a Secretary. How would you like the post?"

"If I were but fitted for it, nothing would make me happier."

"Well, *this* is a sufficient credential," said the Professor, smiling, as he took from the table a paper covered with figures and algebraical symbols.

He then indicated the duties that would devolve upon his Secretary, and stated that the remuneration, to begin with, would be three guineas a week,—a sum that opened up to Alick's imagination a world of possibilities. Contemplating the prospects before him, he almost forgot the pain he would feel at parting from Mrs. Hartmere; but when his excitement had subsided, he turned to thank her for all she had done for him, and to promise to visit her whenever an opportunity offered. " You have taught me," he said, " to look upon you as a mother."

As for Mrs. Hartmere, " this way and that " she " divided her swift mind,"—between grief at his departure, and joy at his good fortune. As the Professor was desirous that Maclean should begin his new work without delay, and it was settled that he should leave for London on the following morning, she had little time before his departure for the indulgence of her sorrows, and kept her gaze steadily fixed on the brighter side of this new phase of things ; for his sake as well as her own. It was with tearless eyes that she embraced him, and with a firm voice that she said Good Bye ; but as soon as he was out of sight, and she had closed the door of her solitary house, her fortitude broke down, and she spent some hours in that silent and subdued agony which is known only to unselfish and loving spirits.
        *   *   *   *   *

Three years have passed by, and we are standing in a darkened room, where a man, still young, though emaciated by illness, is lying on a sick bed, tenderly clasping the hand of a grey-haired woman who sits beside him. Professor Maclean has just recovered from the delirium consequent on a dangerous attack of brain fever, through which he has been nursed tenderly and assiduously by Mrs. Hartmere. As soon as he can be moved, he is to travel southward to some one of the genial watering places of South Devon, and afterwards further change of scene is ordered, as mental labour will be impossible for some months to come. He is paying the penalty which genius so often has to pay when it neglects the dictates of

c

common sense. For a couple of years he worked under Professor Huxtable;—with such ardour and success that, on the Professor's sudden and unexpected death, he was unanimously elected to the vacant chair. He had held it but a few months when the unremitting toil in which day and night he indulged, so weakened his system that a slight chill induced a feverish attack which culminated in inflammation of the brain. For weeks he has hovered on the mysterious confines between life and death. Happily, by an accident, Mrs. Hartmere heard of his dangerous condition, and at once repaired to London. She was in time to prevent his removal to a hospital, and volunteered to take charge of him. He has saved very little money ; and through his illness and convalescence his expenses have been paid by Mrs. Hartmere. It is she who carries him down to Devonshire, and on his complete physical recovery accompanies him to the lakes, and on a tour through Scotland. When he speaks of the pecuniary obligations he is incurring, she declares that she is well able to provide for her adopted son, and that she is simply expending upon him in her lifetime what she has fully intended to have left to him on her death. He cannot do otherwise than accept her generosity, consoling himself with the hope that when he resumes work he shall soon be in a position to repay her.

The time comes, very slowly but surely, when the doctors pronounce that he may safely resume the exercise of his profession. In spite of his intreaties that she will reside with him in London, Mrs. Hartmere then takes leave of him affectionately, and returns to Crayford.

     *   *   *   *   *

Another period of three years has elapsed, and Professor
Maclean pays the first visit to Crayford he has been able to pay
since the summer before his illness.   He is accompanied by his
young wife, to whom he has been very lately married—an
accomplished and charming woman, the daughter of a rich
London merchant, who, beginning by admiring the genius of
the Professor, has ended by loving the virtues and fine
qualities of the man.   You may conjecture the delight with
which he points out to her the various objects of interest in the
quiet old town he once knew so well—the factory, formerly
disused, but recently started again by a limited liability company ; the bank, the town hall, the market-place, Prospect
House, and the steep bridge over the Cray.   At length he turns
down the Winsham Road, and arrives at Hartmere Villa.   For
some months he has not heard from Mrs. Hartmere, and he is
anxious to see her and introduce his wife to her.   To his surprise and pain he soon learns that it is no longer his kind
friend's residence.   After many inquiries he traces her at last to
a little cottage on the Spilsbury Road, a cottage with only two
rooms, and there he finds the noble-hearted woman to whom
he owes so much.   He is shocked beyond measure at perceiving on every side the indications of severe poverty, yet it is
with difficulty he extorts from her a confession of her troubles.
And you can imagine the grief with which he learns that the
expenses of his long illness and gradual recovery were defrayed
from the proceeds of the sale of the Hartmere library.   Yes,
that treasured souvenir of her husband, which she had so often
and so firmly refused to part with, she had sold for the sake
of her adopted son, and had sold it to Mr. Beecham.

On her return to Crayford, after Maclean's recovery, she had been compelled to sell her house, and she was then living on the interest of the purchase money, which Mr. Morton, of Prospect House, had carefully invested for her. Maclean and his wife, however, insisted on her giving up the cottage, and living with them in London. He owed her everything, he said—life, fame, fortune, and happiness—for only her tender and loving assiduity had carried him through his critical illness. He would hear of no excuse and take no refusal, and with glad tears in her eyes, Mrs. Hartmere accompanied Professor and Mrs. Maclean to their handsome house in one of the terraces overlooking the Regent's Park.

*   *   *   *   *

Five years later, and the Professor and his wife again visited Crayford. Mrs. Hartmere went with them, greatly occupied with two lovely children—Alexander Maclean, and Bella Maclean, the younger, who, for some mysterious reason, persisted in calling Mrs. Hartmere "Grandmamma." The old lady still bore the burden of her years with unusual elasticity, and walked with quite a firm step through the well-remembered streets of Crayford. She showed some reluctance when Maclean proposed to have a look at the "old house at home," but did not long oppose her adopted son's earnest request. Her astonishment was beyond bounds when, on arriving at Hartmere Villa, the door opened, and Mr. and Mrs. Maclean entering, led her into the room formerly occupied by her husband. And when she looked around, and saw "the library" once more adorning the old oaken shelves, and had thrust into her hands the deeds which made her once more the owner of Hartmere Villa, her emotion was so intense that it was with difficulty her affectionate friends prevented her from swooning. Excess of joy is sometimes harder to bear than excess of sorrow. The tears rolled down her furrowed cheeks, while her adopted son told her how he had given instructions to Morton, the Crayford solicitor, to let no opportunity pass by of acquiring for him the Hartmere library and Hartmere Villa. Mr. Beecham had been compelled by pecuniary difficulties to dispose of all his property, and Mr. Morton had bought the library privately for the sum Mr. Beecham had originally given for it. The purchaser of Hartmere Villa had removed to London, and was glad to sell the villa for a very moderate sum. As soon as these purchases had been completed, Professor Maclean executed the necessary legal documents for transferring them to Mrs. Hartmere, and thus acquitted himself to some extent of the debt of gratitude he owed to her unselfish friendship. We will not dwell upon the happiness of the old lady during the few remaining years of her well-spent life. It was literally without a cloud, for Mr. and Mrs. Maclean were frequent visitors, and the prattle of their children was as music in her ears, and in her silent hours she refreshed herself with the memories of her married felicity; and at all times she was sustained and cheered by her simple, earnest faith in the mercy of the Divine Father. Full of years and honours she passed away, one hushed Autumn eve, in the peace that passeth understanding; passed away as softly and as calmly as a child lapses into slumber, and, by her desire, her remains were interred in Crayford Churchyard, by the side of her husband. When her will was opened it was found that the Hartmere library and Hartmere Villa had been bequeathed to Professor Alexander Maclean and his heirs for ever, with the proviso that they were always to bear her husband's honoured name.

And thus ends the story of a Wife's Devotion—of a Woman's Self-Sacrifice—and of Love unto Death. For my own part, I never pass Hartmere Villa without raising my hat in homage to the memory of one whose life, both as wife and friend, showed so bright and pure a record.

II.

THE OAKLANDS; OR, COUSIN MARGARET.

 TELL this story in the very words, simple and unadorned, of the young lady from whom I heard it :—

I was growing very tall for my age (said she), and as I showed at the same time signs of weakness, our doctor advised that I should be sent for a few months into the country. As my parents could not then leave London, they accepted for me a kind invitation from some old friends at Crayford; and one fine morning I made my appearance at the Oaklands, and was most hospitably received.

My friends' house was situated on the outskirts of the town; a house with many gables, and tall, twisted chimneys, and ivy-mantled walls, and diamond-panel casements—except in the principal rooms, where modern plate-glass windows had been inserted. Its general aspect was exceedingly picturesque. No doubt it owed something to the effective way in which the surrounding "pleasance" was laid out. Three broad and gradual terraces of turf, adorned with vases full of brilliant flowers, descended to the margin of the little stream of the Cray. To the west stretched a noble garden, rich in the old English blossoms, and glittering with vinery and conservatory.

To the east the house was sheltered by a thick shrubbery and a leafy coppice; while in the rear was situated the well-kept kitchen garden, behind which were a paddock and a bit of pasture—for my friends kept a couple of horses, and three or four cows. You will understand, then, that I had not much cause to regret my temporary exile from my London home.

I could not have visited Crayford at a more delightful season. I have always thought June the loveliest month in the year. May, in our English climate, is so often chilly and uncertain that the promise of Spring frequently remains unfulfilled. In July the cool freshness of the verdure is beginning to pass away, and in August we begin to be aware of the touch of decay on all that is most beautiful around us. Besides, the heat in those two months is sometimes too great to admit of the full and free enjoyment of rural walks.

But in an English June nature is seen at her best and freshest; in all her vigour and vitality, and yet without the over-ripeness of maturity. The air is warm, and yet refreshing; genial, but not enervating. You can spend the whole day out-of-doors without fear of headache. After breakfast you can at once sally forth on your rambles, across warm green meadows and along cool, leafy lanes; and round about Crayford the lanes resemble Arcadian bowers, ash, and oak, and lime bending over them their thick clustering foliage. When you reach the place selected as the goal of your excursion, off go hat and jacket, and you spread your luncheon out upon the fresh green sward, and partake of it with an appetite such as queens, I suspect, can seldom boast of. Then out comes the sketch-book, and the box of colours, and you essay to delineate the fair Crayford landscape, with its crofts and pastures, its long lines of green hedge, where the elder is flowering and the wild rose opening its exquisitely tinted petals, its groups of venerable trees, its sequestered pools, and its grey church-towers, or tall spires, rising above the green shadows of immemorial elms.

Yes, in June, you feel that summer has come, and do not begin to feel that summer is passing. It is the month of roses, which are as closely associated with June as snowdrops with February. The gardens and the copses, the hedgerows and the bowers, are all ablaze with them—white and pink, and red and yellow, large and small, bud and bloom ; roses from the east, and roses from the west ; damask roses, China roses, tea-scented roses, Bourbon roses, Gloire de Dijons, Marèchal Neils, climbing roses, standard roses, dwarf roses ; the humble dog-rose—oh, they are round and about us everywhere, and the air is absolutely heavy with their rich fragrance. Ah me, why do they ever fade ? I think the rose is the *one* flower of which we should never grow weary, which we should rejoice to have with us throughout the whole revolving year. At the Oaklands my friends were very proud, and with good reason, of their roses. They peeped in at the windows when we opened them to admit the morning air ; they climbed over the arbours where we took shelter from the noon-tide heat ; they trailed their lovely blooms above the quaint rustic porch ; they gathered in odorous clusters on the trim parterres, and along the well-kept borders, and everywhere conveyed a sense of unutterable charm and loveliness.

There are few weeks in the year when the fields around Crayford will not reward the pedestrian who wanders among them ; but it is in June they are at their best and brightest. As you then take your way across their grassy breadths, you catch the scent of clover and beans, or the delicate breath of honeysuckle and sweet-briar. The scabious now raises its pretty blossoms; and thrift and valerian, and the azure crow-foot, and the slender campanula, are all a-bloom. The scythe hisses in yonder meadow, or the mowing-machine swings and whirrs, and each sound tells of the levelled grasses which air and sunshine will soon convert into balmy hay. The various kinds which make up the beauty and excellence are said to be—the perennial clover; the yellow goat's-beard; the dog-daisies; the chervil, growing under trees and hedges; the lotus; the yellow rattle; the beautiful quaker-grass, so dear to children; the fragrant fescue; the rough, rude cocksfoot, thriving on banks, and amongst thickets, and in rank grounds; the wild oats and the darnels, which hang their thin red panicles by the wayside; the spiked Timothy and foxtail; the graceful malic; and more abundant, the light, the green, and the purple burnet. All, or almost all, these grasses were to be found in the neighbourhood of Crayford; and you may believe that I had a happy time of it in those sweet summer days at the Oaklands, when a feeling of returning strength enabled me to enjoy everything, and I went about murmuring to myself those pretty verses by Miss Rossetti—

" Winter is cold-hearted;
    Spring is yea and nay;
  Autumn is a weather-cock,
    Blown every way.
  Summer days for me,
  When every leaf is on its tree.

  When Robin's not a beggar,
    And Jenny Wren's a bride,

And larks hang, singing, singing, singing,
  Over the wheat-fields wide,
  And anchored lilies ride,
And the pendulum spider
  Swings from side to side,
And blue-black beetles transact business.
  And gnats fly in a host,
And furry caterpillars hasten
  That no time be lost,
And moths grow fast and thrive,
And lady-birds arrive.

Before green apples blush,
  Before green nuts are brown,
Why, one day in the country
  Is worth a month in town.
  Is worth a day and a year
Of the dusty, musty, lag-last fashion,
  That days drone everywhere."

But I had more than one day in the country. I had many days before me, and I endeavoured to make the most of them while I sojourned with my friends, the Seamores.

Mr. Seamore was the Crayford banker, a man of high character, and a kind host. Mrs. Seamore, a lady of great good-nature, I knew very well, as she had been an occasional visitor at our house in London, where her four children—frolicsome elves, full of life and mischief—were a constant source of anxiety lest their wild and unconsidered movements should endanger the safety of vase, mirror, or ornament. But at the Oaklands, where they were not trammelled by considerations of space, or the exigencies of London fashion, they were sufficiently pleasant companions, and we got on very well together. There was, however, another visitor in the house besides myself; a young lady of rare personal charms, so majestic in her brooding melancholy and slow, languid attitude, that she might have been taken for a fallen queen. Mrs. Seamore called her Katherine; the servants addressed her as Miss Alcester.

Her position in the house impressed me at first as very peculiar, for she evidently ruled it with a rod of iron. Terrible were the reproaches if she were aroused before her usual time by any accidental noise! Great was the indignation if any article she required were not immediately forthcoming! Even good-natured Mrs. Seamore would, under such untoward circumstances, show a little warmth of temper; and Mr. Seamore himself would interfere, though, as a rule, he took little heed of anything that transpired at the Oaklands, apart from his personal affairs. Then, again, nothing was done without consulting her; not a change could be made in the housekeeper's department, or in the gardener's, until her opinion had been asked and obtained. But what struck me most was that certain subjects of conversation were tabooed in her presence. I was constantly hearing Mrs. Seamore—"Oh, do not talk about that, it will wound Katherine!" "We will say nothing about it, lest Katherine should feel pained!" What could all this extraordinary caution mean?

I soon convinced myself that Katherine was a creature of remarkable susceptibility: in truth, she was so sensitive that she was compelled to refrain from doing anything, lest by some mischance it should hurt her feelings. You won't very well come to grief if you never move. At the Oaklands everybody waited upon Miss Alcester, and Miss Alcester did nothing for anybody. Her chief, I think, her sole occupation was to bewail her lot. All day long she kept up a monotonous monologue, of which the constantly recurring phrases were—"When one has suffered as I have done," "When one sees one's self forsaken," "When all one's hopes are shattered," "When there's nothing more in life to wish for," "When one is reduced to live upon charity!" And the conclusion she apparently derived from these undoubtedly gloomy conditions was, that they gave her a right to worry and tyrannize over everybody; a right of which she fully availed herself. Decidedly, thought I, sensitive persons are exceedingly selfish!

One day, when I had been reading to her for an hour or more, while she lay upon a couch by the open window, in the most becoming *negligé* imaginable, I expressed my intention of taking a walk in the garden. You should have heard the extravagant and almost impertinent language in which she addressed me! I left the room with my dignity a good deal ruffled, and was immediately followed by Mrs. Seamore, who overwhelmed me with apologies for what she called Miss Alcester's "constitutional irritability."

"You know, my dear," she said, "she has a claim upon our indulgence; she has been so very unfortunate."

"Unfortunate!" I repeated, with a somewhat incredulous air.

"Oh yes, my dear, most truly unfortunate! She was an orphan, with a large fortune which had been bequeathed to her by her father. The trustee in whose hands he had placed it speculated with and lost it, and shot himself when her approaching marriage to a young nobleman, and the necessary settlements, would have revealed his fraud. The proud girl insisted on breaking off her engagement; 'she would never,' she said, 'enter Lord L.'s family as a pauper;' and she has since lived upon the charity of her friends, and the interest of three or four thousand pounds left to her by her mother. The winter she spends in London, the summer in going from one country-house to another. With us she generally remains for two or three months, since she never seems so happy anywhere else."

I thought to myself that might very well be the case ! Where else would she be so indulged ?

"You see, I knew her when she was a bright, blooming girl, and now talk to her of her youth and her triumphs as an acknowledged belle. Poor Katherine ! it is one of her greatest griefs that her beauty is on the wane."

Here Mrs. Seamore was suddenly interrupted by a sound of voices and merry laughter.

A carriage had driven up to the porch, but the noise of its wheels was lost in the chorus of jubilant exclamations. The merry din filled the hall and ascended the staircase, reaching us where we stood in the corridor, and we could distinguish, amidst the bubbling laughs, and embraces, and joyous cries, the name of "Margaret" repeated by the four little Seamores. "Cousin Margaret ! oh, dear cousin Margaret ! We are *so* glad to see you, Margaret !"

A smile illuminated Mrs. Seamore's countenance.

"My dearest Madge," she exclaimed, and ran down the stairs with the agility of a girl of fifteen.

The children made way for their mother to embrace and welcome the new arrival. I, who had followed Mrs. Seamore with becoming deliberateness, perceived that "Cousin Madge" was a little woman, about forty-five years old, with a plain, even ugly, but expressive face—no, it was not ugly, for the expression was too sweet and tender—and the right shoulder raised much higher than the left. My thoughts immediately glanced from this deformity to the tall and supple figure and regular features of Miss Alcester. But I was recalled to myself by Mrs. Seamore, who hastened to introduce me; and Cousin Madge received me with an air of so much frankness and cordiality, and addressed me in so sweet and musical a voice, that I forgot all about the raised shoulder, and pronounced her to myself one of the most charming women I had ever met.

" A young companion to walk with and try to amuse," said she, as she warmly clasped my hand in her own ; " now, that *is* nice ! I am always ' jolly,' as my brother Tom calls it, at the Oaklands ; but this summer I shall be jollier than ever. How old are you, my child ? Nearly sixteen ! Ah, that is just the age for enjoying rambles in the woods, and pic-nics down by the river. I shall be so pleased if you will join me in some of my excursions. I know every nook and corner for miles round Crayford, and will show you all the pretty bits I have discovered. Are you willing ? "

" Oh, how kind it is of you to ask me ! "

" That is settled, then. You see, my dear," she said, turning towards Mrs. Seamore, " we are friends already."

" Oh, Cousin Margaret, do take *us*, sometimes ! " exclaimed the children.

" Won't you make us a big kite, like the one you made last year ? "

" Take us with you to the farm, and give us some nice cream ! "

" Shall we get up a charade this evening ? "

" No, no, Cousin Margaret, let us sit out on the lawn while you tell us a story."

With a laugh so rich and hearty that it did one good to hear

it, and made one feel inclined to laugh also, she answered,
" Yes, yes, yes ! " to every question.

"They are imposing on you," said Mrs. Seamore at length,
" you must go to your room and rest awhile ; I will send Ellen
to unpack your trunk."

'· No, do not take Ellen from her work. I am not the least
bit tired, and I can unpack my trunk myself. If not, I think I
know where I can find willing assistants. What say you,
children ? "

" Yes, yes, Cousin Margaret, we will help you—oh, do let us
help you ! " and they scampered up the staircase like so many
squirrels. When Miss Nevil—for that was the visitor's name—
with Mrs. Seamore and myself, reached the bedroom, they had
already uncorded the trunk and were looking for the key. This
was produced by Miss Nevil from her reticule, and the trunk
being opened, they stationed themselves around it in joyful
expectancy. Does any pleasure in later life equal the delight
with which a child awaits the forthcoming tip or present ? The
little Seamores knew from experience that their cousin never
forgot them, and they waited with quite a decorous patience for
the good things which this nineteenth century fairy knew so
well how to dispense. In a minute or two their anticipations
were realized : a doll for one, a toy for another, a picture-book
for a third, and a doll's house for a fourth—all the best of their
kind, with many other presents of a more costly and permanent
character, which had evidently been selected with great care,
and with a precise knowledge of the tastes of those for whom
they were intended.

" And how is our poor Katherine ? " enquired Miss Nevil, as
she laid out a charming and valuable coiffure of blonde and

tulle, exquisite in its simplicity, together with a panier of pearls of exquisitely simple design. "These, I think, will just suit her, and harmonize with her style of beauty. She likes to dress well, I think, and she is handsome enough to do so."

"She cannot fail to be pleased, my dear, with so charming a gift. Margaret, you think of everybody but yourself! As for Katherine's health, it seems pretty good, but her spirits are very low. She is not able, even now, to forget the past, and the depression which weighs upon her she seems unable to throw off. We must be patient with her, Margaret. As she says of herself, her nature is like an Æolian harp, which responds to the breath of every wind. But, Margaret, since your pupil is on the eve of being married, you are free, are you not?"

"Free as the air! and I don't mean to take another pupil, as my means are now sufficient for my wants; I intend to spend my time without regard for the utilities!"

"Then I lay an embargo on you, my dear cousin, for ever and ever. You cannot, you will not refuse me; help me to bring up these noisy children to be as good and as unselfish as yourself. The girls are as bad as the boys through their always being together, and their governess can do nothing with them."

"If I can educate them to be like their mother," replied Cousin Margaret, with a smile, "I shall be well satisfied. I think I did very well with *you*, my dear."

"Since cousin is going to stay with us," exclaimed Emma, the youngest, "we will keep to-day as a great holiday, and I will ask cook to make us a fine cake for tea in the nursery."

Away she hastened, followed by the others; and I could hear them informing the cook, and the housemaids, and the gardener, and the groom, that Cousin Margaret had come, and was not

D

going away again for years and years. Afterwards I found that
Miss Nevil was as great a favourite with the servants as with
everybody else. The good opinion of servants I consider a
valuable testimonial ; for they are keen critics, and as impartial
as they are keen. Moreover, they see us as we are, for one
seldom thinks of wearing a mask in the presence of one's
servants.

When I came to know Miss Nevil I ceased to wonder that
everybody liked her. She was gifted with a singularly sweet
temper, with the most unselfish nature I ever met, and with
an inexhaustible vivacity. You always felt the happier and the
better for being in her company. She was one of those
admirable creatures who seem specially sent by Heaven to light
up with a glow of sunshine the dreariness of our ordinary
existence. Her treatment of Miss Alcester was very ingenious.
She never showed her any pity, never spoke to her of her
troubles, but made her forget them ; somehow or other she
always contrived to lead her thoughts away from the subject,
herself, on which they usually brooded. As for the little Seamores, they loved her passionately ; without any apparent effort
she kept them in harmony and good temper ; and they caught
from her something of her own tone of fine breeding. Their
governess declared that they no longer caused her the least
anxiety ; their lessons were almost always well done ; and their
behaviour had so improved that she had really little to complain of.

It is wonderful the influence for good a woman like Miss
Nevil can exercise in a household. I must confess that I
worshipped her as a being of a superior order, and did my best
to imitate her, while feeling she was inimitable. I was
astonished at the range of her information, at the versatility

of her talents; but, perhaps, most of all, at her inexhaustible goodness and unfailing gaiety. Deformed, and yet so bright ! To me it seemed that had I been similarly afflicted, I should have sunk into a condition of chronic despondency. One day I chanced, in conversing with Mrs. Seamore, to refer compassionately to Cousin Margaret's misfortune. She looked at me with mild surprise, and after a minute's pause, exclaimed—

"My dear Lily "—have I told you my name ? It was Lily Hawthorne before I married—" Cousin Margaret has always been the same light-hearted, happy creature ever since I knew her, and that was many years ago, for she brought me up from my childhood. Nobody ever thinks about what you call her deformity, or thinks of pitying her, because she never pities herself. I assure you she enjoys life thoroughly, and I don't know that she has ever wished to be other than she is."

Whether Cousin Margaret overheard us or not, I cannot determine ; but next day, when I was sitting with head and shoulders bent over my book, she laughingly drew me erect, as she stood behind me, and said, " Come, Miss Hawthorne, keep yourself as straight as an arrow ; if you stoop at your age you run the risk of becoming a hunchback, like myself, and that you know is not pretty."

I blushed to the roots of my hair at hearing the offensive word upon her dear lips. She began to laugh. "Oh, my dear child, do not blush on my account ; it is not worth the trouble. Long ago I made up my mind to bear my cross with a light heart. I have so many blessings to thank God for, that I should be ungrateful, indeed, if I grieved over a solitary crumpled rose-leaf, which, after all, has proved a blessing in disguise ; for it has sobered my extravagant spirits, restrained my self-conceit, and forced me to look—as without it I should never have looked—at the serious side of life."

Soon afterwards she left me to reflect upon her thoughtful words. I was interrupted in my not unpleasant meditations by the entrance of Mrs. Seamore, who, with a pale face and trembling lips, sat down beside me, threw her arms round my waist, and sobbing out, " My dearest child, my poor, dear Lily ! " handed me a letter. It was in my mother's handwriting. I read it eagerly, and, oh, with such a dull, dead pain at the heart ! For it conveyed the startling intelligence that my father having, by an unlucky speculation, lost nearly all his capital, was compelled to give up his establishment in London, and retire to a small town in Lanarkshire, near which, a year or two ago, he had erected some experimental works on a limited scale.

At fifteen years of age one does not brood very long over the sorrows of life ; and as soon as the first shock had spent its force, I began to reconstruct my father's fortune with novel and surprising efforts of the imagination. No doubt I should soon have accustomed myself to look on the brighter aspect of things, but for the inopportune sympathy of Mrs. Seamore, and the condolences of Miss Alcester, who found a melancholy satisfaction in comparing my fate with her own, and deduced from the comparison, with the usual lamentations over *her* past, the most dismal prognostications as to *my* future. I naturally began to feel that I was an exceedingly ill-used individual, deserving of the pity of the whole universe ; and, retiring to my room, I threw myself on my bed in a passion of tears, and lay awake half the night, convinced that I was broken-hearted.

Next morning my aching eyes, after a few hours of broken

and uneasy slumber, opened on the two things best calculated
to cheer and encourage me—the bright, golden sunshine, which
always acted on my nerves like a tonic, and Cousin Margaret's
kindly voice and sympathetic gaze.   She smiled upon me and
embraced me, and without appearing to notice my reddened
eyelids and swollen face, took from her pocket a small copy of
the New Testament, and read a chapter aloud in her soft and
soothing voice.   Then she said, in her cheeriest tones, "See,
Lily, what a lovely morning it is !   Would you like to breakfast
with me at Simpson's farm, lower down the river ?   It is a good
walk, but as we shall not take the children with us, you and I
will soon cover the distance."

She assisted me to dress, and in twenty minutes we were
both of us stepping briskly through the woods on our way to
Mr. Simpson's farm.

I remember to this day the exquisite delight of that morning
walk.   In the calm of the early hours of day my troubled spirit
found repose, and my mind could not dwell upon gloomy ideas
when all around me was so bright and joyous.   A thousand
things diverted my attention—the play of light through the
meshwork of the branches, the songs of thrush and blackbird
from the secure depths of the thickets, of the chiff-chaff from the
hedge, and the lark in the blue air above, the scamper of a
flurried hare across the sward, the rustle of the bracken as we
pressed through it up to our knees, the ceaseless murmur of
insects happy in their ephemeral existence.   The pathways
wandered in and out and crossed one another like a maze, but
the plash of the river against its pebbly bank guided us in our
course, and before long we came in sight of its shining ripples,
and followed it closely until we arrived at Oakden Farm.

Mrs. Simpson received us cordially. It appeared that in her summer visits to the Oaklands Miss Nevil was accustomed to take frequent excursions in this direction, always stopping at the farm for breakfast or tea, according as her excursions were made in the morning or the evening. She requested Mrs. Simpson to prepare breakfast for two, and while it was getting ready carried me off into the orchard, where she made me sit down in the shade of a mossy-apple tree, seemingly of patriarchal dignity.

"And now, my dear Lily, open your heart to me," she said. "I would not speak to you yesterday, because your grief was too fresh and your excitement too great. Now that you are more composed, and we are alone, I shall be pleased if you will take me into your confidence."

"Oh, yes! and if you, too, should pity me—should compassionate me—dear Miss Nevil, how thankful I shall feel! It added to my grief to think that you alone cared nothing for my misfortune."

"If you wish it, I will certainly pity you; but first let us consider whether there is any need for so much display of emotion. What, after all, *is* this heavy affliction of yours, which has cost you a sleepless night? Let us look it in the face, and see what stuff it is made of. Half the bogeys in the world are only sham bogeys, as you soon discover if you look them firmly in the face. They are like those banks of cloud which the sailor catches sight of in the distance and mistakes for ranges of iron-bound cliffs, but steering his ship right on to them they vanish away, and prove to have been but mist and vapour after all."

Judge of my surprise at this seemingly cold indifference!

For a moment I felt disposed to be silent in the face of so much hard-heartedness; it needed all my pride and resolution to keep back my tears. At length I faltered out, with half a sob,

"Don't you know—that my fa—ther—has lost—an im—mense sum—of—mon—ey?"

Here I grew a little calmer and contrived to speak connectedly.

"And that I shall have to leave Warwick Square and all. my friends? and go away to a dirty little Scotch town, where I know nobody, and everything is ugly and detestable? Imagine, dear Miss Nevil, what I shall feel at seeing no more the Parks, and Regent Street, and the Gardens! Can you, can you conceive anything more deplorable?"

"Easily! Believe me, Lily, you will soon learn to love other scenes and to make new friendships, if you do not obstinately wrap yourself up in the conviction that you are a crushed and heart-broken individual—as limp as Mr. Mantalini in Dickens's novel! This is a common enough form of vanity, and a very unpleasant one. Now, if I am to share my sympathy with anybody it will be with your father and mother, whom, by the way, you seem to have quite forgotten."

"Oh! my poor parents!" I exclaimed, in some confusion; "Yes, it will be a terrible blow for them, will it not? Poor mother, how hard it will be upon her! Yes, I feel for them, my dear Miss Nevil, and more than I do for myself." . . . And really, for the moment, this was true—Miss Nevil's words having recalled me from my egotistical lamentations.

"And, meanwhile, their sole thought and concern will be for *you*. Ah, Lily, do not let us talk about pity and compassion, except for them. You are much happier than they,

or should be, because it will be in your power to console them.
The joy of all joys is to be able to help others. I often think
how happy our Lord Jesus must be, knowing that He has the
power and the will to save souls! If your parents see you
with a cheerful countenance, adapting yourself to the new
conditions of your lot, they will soon forget their reverses, or,
at least, will cease to dwell upon them, and will pluck up
heart and courage to endeavour to retrieve their losses. And
now you know why I did not join yesterday evening in the
chorus of pity that wailed around you. It was no kindness to
unnerve and soften you; what you wanted was to be braced
up and strengthened in good resolves and brave purposes.
Oh! Lily, I will not believe that yours is a coward's spirit;
I will not believe that you lack the courage to do your duty,
when you understand what your duty is."

"Thank you, dear Miss Nevil," I replied, pressing her hand
warmly, "you do me more good than Miss Alcester. I see
now how selfish I was in all my trouble yesterday—it was
all for myself, what *I* should lose, what *I* should suffer!
And—do you know?—I think Miss Alcester was selfish, too,
and that she was thinking of herself all the time she was pro-
fessing to be sorry for me. But I will not blame her, for
everybody says she has been most unfortunate."

"Yes," replied Miss Nevil gravely, "unfortunate indeed,
because her misfortune was of her own making. You look
surprised. Well, I will briefly tell her story as we return to
the Farm, where breakfast by this time must be ready. Miss
Alcester was gifted with great beauty, a splendid voice, and
an artist's genius; and these rare gifts were her ruin. I knew
her when she was a child, and a spoiled child; nothing was

handsome enough or good enough for Kate ; her poor mother was unwise enough to encourage her in her love of show and adulation. She was younger than you when she was introduced into Society, where her beauty and her wealth procured her a host of admirers, and the compliments showered upon her completely turned her head. Her musical accomplishments were exceptional, and helped to win the notoriety which she loved. To cultivate her mind seemed unnecessary, when her most vapid remark was caught up and repeated as if it had embodied a wise thought, or sparkled with a flash of wit. Her parents grew alarmed at the wayward and audacious course she was pursuing, and at length succeeded in concluding an engagement between their daughter and a young nobleman of high character, Lord L. But soon after the betrothal Mr. Alcester, who had plunged into some gigantic speculations, was taken ill quite suddenly, and in two days was a corpse. His guiding brain withdrawn, his affairs became inextricably involved, and Katherine Alcester found herself almost penniless. Her fiancé, however, like a man of honour, was prepared to fulfil his engagement ; when, chancing to hear her disputing with her mother the control of the little income saved from the wreck of her husband's fortune, he was led to make some sharp remonstrance. Miss Alcester's haughty temper broke forth in a storm of angry words, and she accused him of having always wished to marry not her, but her money, and of seeking a pretext to withdraw from an undesirable position. ' Go !' she exclaimed, 'and let me never see you again.' I have no doubt that she immediately regretted her violence ; but she was too proud to own it, and the marriage never took place.

"Many friends interested themselves in Mrs. Alcester and

her daughter ; and it was suggested that Katherine might turn to account her talents as a musician. This, she declared, was an insupportable degradation. Mr. Alcester's daughter could never become a teacher. Her mother's relatives then subscribed a sum to purchase an annuity, which, added to the small sum I have already spoken of, would insure them a respectable livelihood ; but since her mother's death she has preferred to live upon her friends, spending a month here, and a month there, and always posing as the martyr to an untoward Destiny, when she is really the victim of her own ungoverned passions.

"Perhaps I speak severely ; but it is painful to see a life so sadly wasted, which was capable of better things. I am telling you this story, remember, that you yourself may profit by it, and learn, above all things, to subdue a selfish and egotistical spirit. Self is the rock on which so many a gallant vessel is wrecked at the very outset of life's voyage. Do you, my dear Lily, want to be pitied as Miss Alcester is pitied? Do you want the same kind of almost contemptuous compassion—the indulgence too often extended to a spoiled child—expended upon you? Will you not rather seek to live an honourable life of independence, doing your duty bravely in whatever circumstances the will of God may place you ?"

"I will, indeed I will," was my answer. "I will try to do my duty always, and to be content with my lot, whatever that may be. When I get back to the Oaklands I will at once write home, and ask if I may return, and give what help I can."

"Well said, Lily, and I hope I may say, by-and-bye, well done. But we are neglecting Mrs. Simpson's nice breakfast, and she will feel aggrieved if we do not do justice to her fresh milk and newly-made butter, and eggs, and bacon—all off the farm. Say grace, my dear, and then prove that your morning walk has not spoiled your appetite."

I soon proved this to Miss Nevil's entire satisfaction, and I do not know when I ever enjoyed a meal more. The cream, the butter, the eggs, the bacon—all seemed "extra good," and I think Mrs. Simpson had no cause to complain that they were not appreciated. When Miss Nevil had paid her very moderate charges, and thanked her for her kind attention, we started on our return journey, but by a different route, and arrived at the Oaklands just as Miss Alcester made her first appearance for the day.

When I had written my letter to my mother, I accompanied Miss Nevil into the garden, and while she was making some garments for a poor woman in the neighbourhood, who had lost her husband, and was left with a large family to bring up, I read to her from one of her favourite books. I remember that I came to a beautiful sonnet by Mr. Aubrey de Vere, beginning thus—

> " Count each affliction, whether light or grave,
> God's messenger sent down to thee; do thou
> With courtesy receive him ; rise and bow ;
> And, ere his shadow pass thy threshold, crave
> Permission first his heavenly feet to lave."

When I had read these lines I involuntarily paused ; for the thought occurred to me that it was in just this spirit Miss Nevil had confronted *her* affliction. Observing my silence, she asked me playfully what I was thinking of. I told her as well as I could, and with a sigh she answered—"I fear I have not always been submissive, and sometimes I have found the cross very hard to bear. But I will tell you *my* story, as I have told

you Miss Alcester's, though I confess I do not care to talk
about myself   There is nothing wonderful in it, but the story
of the most commonplace life cannot fail to carry a lesson with
it, a warning or an example.

"I suppose I was rather pretty in my infancy. Everybody
around me said so, and I soon learned to be pleased with the
compliment. My father, as you may have heard, was a
Government official, occupying an influential position, and as
his income was a good one, and my mother had brought him a
small landed property in Ireland, we lived in good style—a
house at the West End, carriage, servants, etc. They had but
three children, myself, and another daughter, and a son, both
younger than me by some years. We were a very happy family,
and my first grief was the death of my good, kind father.

"My sister Louisa was then about six years old, and my
brother Edgar, four. We were of course compelled to reduce
our establishment considerably; but my mother was a good
manager, and contrived to make a limited income supply us·
with all reasonable comforts. I gave her all the help of which
I was capable; and being very fond of books I pursued my
studies with a good deal of enthusiasm, and made what I
suppose was satisfactory progress. A twelvemonth passed very
quickly, but towards the end of it I observed that my mother
frequently glanced at me with an anxious and disturbed look.

"One day a physician of high repute called upon us—I afterwards found by appointment—and being introduced into our
school-room, took special notice of myself, because, I supposed,
I was the eldest, and manipulated my back and shoulders a
good deal. As he left the room he observed, 'Oh, it will be
nothing!' But my mother went downstairs with him, was

absent for some minutes, and when she returned I remarked that she had been shedding tears. A week later she told me that my figure was growing crooked, that steps must be taken at once to prevent further curvature of the spine, and that for this purpose she had arranged to place me under the care for a time of an experienced surgeon. I had begun to be sensible of some physical discomfort, and had quite enough of the woman in me to wish to preserve my good looks and good figure. So you may be sure I offered no objection, and, as a matter of fact, should not have ventured to do so, if I had felt any, as my mother, with all her affection, insisted on prompt obedience.

"Well, I remained a year in the surgeon's establishment, undergoing a very painful course of treatment, which, unfortunately, led to no good result. On the contrary, I was much more deformed, and any beauty I had once possessed suffering had completely destroyed. My return home, you may be sure, was but a melancholy affair. My mother wept very much at my altered appearance, while I could scarcely restrain my tears when I looked upon her. You know that the troubles in Ireland fell very heavily on families who were entirely dependent on the rents from their estates. So little had been paid by my mother's tenants that she had experienced the greatest difficulty in making both ends meet, especially as she had to pay a heavy sum for my board, lodging, and surgical treatment. She had removed to a small house in a street in Pimlico, and kept but one servant, practising every economy she could devise so as to keep out of debt. The struggle proved too much for her, and a few months after my return home she died, prematurely worn out.

"Ah, what a responsibility then devolved on my deformed shoulders! At fifteen years of age I was an orphan and the

head of a family, for Louisa and Edgar had only me to depend
upon. A cousin of my father's, the mother of dear Mrs. Seamore, who was then a child, took charge of us, and under her
hospitable roof I resumed my studies with all the energy I could
command, determined not to grieve over what could not be
undone, and by always wearing a lively countenance and maintaining a cheerful demeanour, to prevent people from pitying
me, which, somehow or other, I felt to be humiliating. My
cousin was exceedingly kind; but her husband, though not a
bad-hearted man, sometimes made me feel that he supported
three strangers with a good deal of reluctance. I made haste
to pass the Local Examinations, and having fortunately carried
off honours, felt able to propose that I should undertake the
education of my little cousin as a set-off against the cost of the
maintenance of myself and my two dear charges. The proposal
was accepted, and for eight years I educated Mrs. Seamore,
together with my sister Louisa.

"Edgar had obtained an exhibition at the Grammar School,
and as I was anxious he should go from there to the University,
I sought another situation, where the salary would enable me
to assist in his support. But I still kept up my affectionate
relations with my cousins, and spent my holidays with them.
Then I met with Professor B., who was an almost daily visitor,
and we got into the habit of conversing very freely together,
and pleasant—too pleasant—I found those conversations.

"In my next holidays, however, I found that the Professor
no longer conversed with me, but with my charming Louisa,
who had blossomed out into a beautiful and refined young
woman. At first, I felt a bitter pang; but I soon remembered that I was deformed and unlovely, and then Louisa

was not only my sister, but my pupil, and I was not only fond, but proud, of her. When she told me that she was engaged to the Professor—a young and handsome man, my dear, though so learned—I was as delighted as her mother, if living, would have been. But, ah me! what troubles came upon me in later years. After a brief enjoyment of happy married life my Louisa died in giving birth to her first child. Edgar distinguished himself at the University, took holy orders, joined the Central African Mission, and perished of the terrible African fever.

"No, I have not always been submissive; I have sometimes repined when I have felt that I was alone in this great cold world, but then I have remembered that it was God's will, and have tried to 'count each affliction, whether light or grave,' as a Divine messenger sent down to me, and I have sought happiness, my dear, in doing my duty as best I can, trusting in God to give me the needful strength.

"Such is the story of my life, dear Lily. I told you there was nothing remarkable in it. Like other lives, it has had its afflictions; but, like other lives, it has had its bright intervals of sunshine. I try to think that there is more sunshine than cloud, and to preserve a spirit of contentment and cheerfulness. . . . but I have talked too much and too long about myself, and daresay I have made out that I am quite a heroine, instead of what I really am, a very plain and common-place individual—'Cousin Margaret,' at your service!"

*   *   *   *   *

Two years afterwards, at my mother's request, Cousin Margaret paid us a visit at our new home in the West of Scotland. She found me engaged in teaching a class of the factory children to read, in superintending a clothing club, and a penny bank, and a Sunday school, and in other work of the same unpresuming, but, I hope, not unprofitable character. I had found a vocation in life, and it interested me greatly. It also interested Cousin Margaret, who gave me some sound advice on several points of importance. We enjoyed her sojourn with us amazingly, making excursions to the various beautiful scenes in the neighbourhood, and spending a day or two at Glasgow and Edinburgh. I told her of all that had been accomplished in the two years; that my father had succeeded beyond his hopes, that my mother had recovered her health and spirits, and that I felt no desire to return to Paris. And I added that all my happiness and all my desire to be useful were due to the kind, nice words which, in the hour of need, had opportunely been spoken by

COUSIN MARGARET.

III.

REDLEAF HOUSE ; OR, HUSBAND AND WIFE.

MR. and Mrs. Mortimer were among the richest and most influential of the Crayford residents. They occupied a large and spacious mansion on the outskirts of the town, surrounded by extensive gardens, plantations, and meadow-land, " all enclosed," as the advertisements say, " in a ring fence." It was known as Redleaf House, perhaps from the autumn-tints of a gigantic Virginia creeper which covered one side of the house with its spreading foliage.

One day Mrs. Mortimer, who had driven into the town to do some "shopping," dismissed her carriage, and informed her footman that she would walk home. She was detained by her various errands much longer than she had expected ; and, when the last was completed, observing unmistakeable signs of a shower, resolved on taking a short cut homeward through the Well Lane, a narrow and squalid thoroughfare which the ladies of Crayford, except as district visitors or tract distributors, seldom cared to visit. Just as she reached it the rain began to come down heavily. Now Mrs. Mortimer was radiant in a summer attire of the airiest and brightest character, and wore on her head a "ravishing" little bonnet, all tulle, and lace, and ribbons, and flowers, which her pink silk parasol could not

E

prevent from utter ruin. What should she do? That marvel
of a bonnet! That new mantle! That dainty costume! All
would be destroyed; and as she was sensible that they were
particularly becoming, their destruction she could not contemplate with equanimity. Fortunately, she caught sight on the
other side of the lane of an old gateway, opening into a kind
of yard, which offered a welcome shelter. In a moment she
had taken advantage of it; though, to be sure, the gateway
was so old and dirty, and the enclosed space behind it so dreary-
looking and dismal, that she did not feel at all comfortable,
and regretted that she had so hastily dismissed her carriage.

She was musing on the ill-luck which had brought down a
pelt of rain on the first afternoon she had chosen for a walk,
when her attention was suddenly arrested by a sound of voices—
and angry voices too—proceeding from the ground floor of a
dilapidated-looking house just inside the yard.

"Go to the 'Spread Eagle' then, you sot!" screamed a
woman's voice, "go and drink away your children's bread,
you brute!"

"Yes, all right, I'm off," answered a man's voice, "and I
don't mean to return as long as I have the price of a pint of
porter in my pocket. Who the d ——l wants to stay under the
same roof with a cantankerous old hag like you, who can't
keep a civil tongue in your head for five minutes together, and
worry the life out of a man with your incessant clacking?"

"Civil tongue, indeed! And who are you that I should keep
a civil tongue in my head for? Do you ever spend an evening
at home with your own wife and children? Ar'n't you down
every night at that 'Spread Eagle' with Jerry Brown and Tom
Smith, and the rest of the idle lot?"

"And who has driven me there? I was as good a husband and as steady a workman as ever was seen in Crayford when we were first married ! But you—pah !—you've been an idle baggage always; you can't even handle a needle like other women ! look at my clothes—full of holes because you are too lazy to darn 'em, and as for the children, they're bundles of rags and tatters. When I come home—home? dash it all, how can you call it a home ?—everything is sixes and sevens, and as black as my hat ; and there's not a bite or a sup to be had, for the fire's gone out while you've been gossiping at old Mother Fergusson's. Is it any wonder I go to the 'Spread Eagle ?' I should be a fool if I stayed here !"

And slamming the door, the man came out into the gateway, passed Mrs. Mortimer, apparently without noticing her, and sauntered forth into the wet and muddy street. She perceived that he was still young, and that his countenance was worn by trouble rather than brutalized by drink. He stooped as he went, as if he had not strength to hold himself erect. His clothes were shabby, but there was something in their style and in the way they were worn which, to an experienced eye, showed that their wearer had been accustomed to better days. Mrs. Mortimer, however, was not accustomed to take heed of such signs, and involved him and his class in the one sweeping censure which the rich are fond of pronouncing on the poor : "They are all alike," she said; "all these men of the lower orders. They spend in drink the wages they ought to give to their wives—and such good wages, too ! As much, I am told, as thirty and thirty-five shillings a week ! How *can* they go and spend so much money in those dreadful public-houses !"

But at this moment Mrs. Mortimer's thoughts were diverted from the iniquities of the British workman by the appearance of three little children, who had toddled out after their father, and began to amuse themselves by making mud-pies in the gutter. Such dirty, untidy, ragged children she thought she had never seen before, though it is true that her acquaintance with the children of the poor was exceedingly limited. Their clothes were filthy and in rags, their hair seemed not to have been combed for weeks, the accumulated dirt of days begrimed their hands and faces. Mrs. Mortimer was indignant. "The poor man," she said to herself, "is to be pitied after all. The mother who would let her children go about in such a condition cannot be a good wife. Of course, her husband ought *not* to go to the 'Spread Eagle;' but a home with three such little wretches as these in it must be the reverse of inviting."

As the rain continued, Mrs. Mortimer yielded to a sudden impulse, turned up the yard, and through the open door looked into the room just quitted by the children and their father. In her soft and luxurious existence she had hardly ever seen such a sight, and it set her thinking. There were two bedsteads in the room, the frame of one of which was broken, so that a stool had been used to prop it up. The walls were so black with smoke and dirt and grease that it was impossible to say whether they were painted or papered. In the middle of the room stood a table as black as the walls, on which were two or three empty plates, a couple of cups, each without a handle, an old knife and fork, and a plate with three or four crusts upon it. The fire was smouldering in the grate, and opposite to it, on a wooden chair—there was only one other in the room—sat the workman's wife, her elbows on her knees, and her face between her two hands, staring at vacancy, and sometimes with a toss throwing her elf-locks off her forehead.

After a moment's hesitation, Mrs. Mortimer entered.

"My good woman," she said, "can you shelter me from the rain for a few minutes?"

The woman gazed with surprise on the richly-dressed lady before her. Rising, she made a kind of curtsey, and offered the chair on which she had been sitting, first wiping it with her apron. "Yes, ma'am, of course, ma'am; but this is not the place for a lady like you, ma'am."

"What is your name, my good woman?"

"Name? oh, Hepzibah Johnson—Johnson's my husband's name—worse luck for me that ever I heard it!"

"I am sorry to hear you say *that*, Mrs. Johnson. What is your husband's trade?"

"He's a carpenter, ma'am, and a very good workman when he's sober—which he isn't half as often as he ought to be. It's all the drink, ma'am. He can make good wages, and might keep me and the children quite respectable and genteel-like; but he goes off in the evenings, ma'am, to the 'Spread Eagle,' ma'am—that's the public-house round the corner—and there his mates get him to treat them, for he's soft and good-natured is Johnson."

"But don't you think, Mrs. Johnson, you might keep him at home if you tried?"

"Tried, ma'am? I *have* tried. I have scolded him, ma'am, and shown him up before his mates, and done everything I could to prevent him from going a-drinking with Tom Smith and Jerry Brown, and the rest of 'em, but it's of no use."

"Well, Mrs. Johnson, the rain has stopped I see, and I must

thank you for accommodating me.   I am Mrs. Mortimer, of
Redleaf House, and I will make some enquiries about you,
Johnson, and see if anything can be done for you."

"Oh, ma'am ; if you can make Johnson save his wages and
stay at home with his wife and children, I will humbly thank
you."

"Well, we shall see.   But if I were you I would tidy the
children, and clean and put this room in order, and then I think
Johnson would not go so often to the 'Spread Eagle.'   Here is
a shilling for you ; " and without waiting to hear Mrs. Johnson's
expressions of gratitude, she passed quickly into the street, and
returned to Redleaf House without further adventure.

"Has your master returned?" she inquired of her maid as
she entered her dressing-room.

" He has been in, ma'am, but he went out again, saying he
should be back at seven to dinner, and that cook must be very
punctual, as at nine he had an engagement at his club."

· "His club!" murmured young Mrs. Mortimer to herself.
" He is there every evening now, yet when we were first married
he seldom went from home.   In our rank of life the club is as
seductive to husbands as the public-house is among the poor."

Removing her bonnet and mantle, and making some changes
in her attire, Mrs. Mortimer dismissed her maid, and sat down
to have, what a little friend of mine calls, " a good thinking."
From the shade on her brow and the quiver of her beautiful
lips, it was evident that her reflections were not of a peculiarly
cheerful nature.   There are moments in life when the memories
of bye-gone days rise unbidden before us, and compel us to
retrace our way through the shadowy corridors of the Past,
however unwelcome to us may be the retrospect.

It was so with Mrs. Mortimer. She saw herself as only eight years before, a beautiful bride of nineteen summers she had entered her house for the first time leaning on her husband's arm, and looking up with happy pride into his smiling face. She recalled the early years of her married life, her husband's fond attentions, the walks and drives they took together, the evenings they spent in each other's society, then the birth of her children, and her happiness as a young mother, all the tender little episodes in which her children figured—and as she recalled these things she sighed deeply, and the tears gathered in her eyes. Yet why should it be so? In these scenes of memory's kaleidoscope there was nothing to awaken regret. In truth, so far her life had been spent amid the sunshine and the roses; no clouds had darkened it; no noxious weeds had sprung up in her path; she had been blessed with unusual prosperity; even her children had been spared many of the trials of childhood; and yet she sighed still more deeply, and the tears glided down the smooth curves of her fair young cheeks as she murmured—

"Then, then, I was happy; but now——"

She began to reflect. Since that period of wedded bliss a great change had taken place; gradually, a dark shadow had folded over the scene; but whence came that shadow? What was the cause of it? Only a few short years ago her husband and she seemed to have but one will, one thought, one object and joy in life; and now she felt with a pang that she stood alone—that the husband, in whose strength she had confided, had stepped aside, and she was left to tread life's difficult path without his helping hand. Why was this? What did it all mean? These were questions she could not answer; but, shuddering, she recognized the fact that she and her husband were almost as surely parted in their affections as the miserable man and his scolding wife in the dismal alley she had lately visited. Mr. Mortimer went his own way, and she went hers; their pursuits, their pleasures, their tastes were different; they were separated by an invisible, but very real barrier.

Again she asked herself how it was that her husband, who formerly begrudged every hour he was compelled to spend from home, now begrudged, apparently, every hour which he spent under his own roof. He still loved his children, it was true, and would still take them on his knee, and tell them the fanciful stories he knew so well how to invent; but as soon as their bedtime came he immediately withdrew to his club or to a friend's, unless, indeed, he preferred the seclusion of his library. Of course, when a dinner party or a ball was given, he played his part as host with his usual courtesy; and duly attended his wife to the various social "functions" at which their presence was expected. But this was all. And Mrs. Mortimer, in like manner, pursued an independent, or rather a separate course; had her own amusements, her morning calls, her shopping excursions, her drives, her five o'clock teas, and her cozy evening parties.

In vain Mrs. Mortimer endeavoured to discover the cause. It was his club, it was his friends, it was the society he frequented; but in her heart of hearts she felt and knew that it was neither. No; she could not arrive at any satisfactory conclusion, because as yet her eyes had not been opened to the fact that the cause was in herself.

A babble of childish voices aroused her, of voices raised in anger and contention. She hastened to the nursery, where Frank, the youngest, who was unable to walk without help, had caught hold of the dress of Clara to steady his tottering steps. That young lady happened at the time to be very busy with her doll, and, fearing her frock would be torn, had pushed him aside so violently that he fell full-length upon the carpet. Her elder brother George, in resentment at such harsh treatment of the child, had snatched her doll away from her, and thrown it under the grate. Result : angry words exchanged between George and Clara, and loud cries from Baby Frank.

"Where can Kate be?" said Mrs. Mortimer, astonished at the scene before her. "Why has she left these children alone? Some terrible accident might have happened!" And she rang the nursery bell. A moment's examination satisfied her that the baby was not hurt, and she soon kissed away his tears; while in their mother's presence George and Clara suspended hostilities.

When Kate made her appearance she received a severe scolding, and was reminded of all the possible catastrophes that might have occurred in her absence. The children might have been burned to death, might have fallen downstairs, might have climbed on the chairs to look out of the window and overbalanced themselves, might have—

"Yes, ma'am," interrupted Kate, rather flippantly, "but nothing *ever* has happened to them, ma'am, though "—in a lower voice—" 'tisn't often *you* trouble about them ! "

Mrs. Mortimer, who overheard the saucy speech, was inclined to dismiss her on the spot, but she remembered that she would have the trouble of engaging another to fill her place. She contented herself, therefore, with reprimanding her sharply, and bidding the children good-night, went down to dinner.

About eight o'clock her husband went out as usual, and Mrs.

Mortimer sat down in her splendid drawing-room to spend the evening alone. She took up a book, but tired of it after reading a few pages, and threw it aside. The piano did not satisfy her; she pronounced it out of tune. She turned to her embroidery, but wearying of it immediately, selected the most luxurious easy chair in the room, threw herself into it, with her feet on a velvet footstool, and through the open window gazed on the sunset-glories of the summer sky.

"How tired and dull I feel!" she exclaimed, "I wish I had accepted Mrs. Hartmere's invitation, for then my husband would have accompanied me. He likes to talk with Mr. Hartmere about his beloved books and experiments. Heigh-ho! It seems strange that the only way I can get George's company is by going out. He is never at home, that is certain. It is shameful; it is cruel. I wonder whether any other wife in Crayford is so badly treated as I am!"

She made an effort to sleep, but, as is often the case, had never felt more wakeful. The events of the day had excited her, and started her mind on a train of thought she had hitherto refused to follow. The voice of her conscience spoke in tones that seemed to demand her attention. "You throw the blame," it said, "on your husband; but are you sure that you are not more deserving of it? When he married you, do you not think he expected to find in you a woman of firmer character, with graver interests in life, more attached to her home, more constant in the discharge of her duties? We will not say that you do any evil; but ask your own heart, do you do any good? And if one does not do the good one might and could do, is not that almost the same as doing evil?

"You regret the happy days of your early wedded life, when

you and your husband were all in all to each other, with the same
interests, the same aims, the same pleasures; but that these have
passed away are not you to blame?   Did you not involve yourself
in all the whirl and din of Society, for which you knew he had
little liking?   Were you not aware that when he attended you
to a ball it was with a desire to gratify your wishes, and at a great
sacrifice of his own?   But while you fluttered from one gay
scene to another, you forgot that you were destroying in him
as well as in yourself the *home habits* and the enjoyment of
domestic pleasures ?   For the pastimes and pursuits of fashion
you have neglected the cultivation of your mind, the development of your highest faculties.

"Suppose that your husband had spent this evening with
you, on what subjects could you converse?   People must
necessarily talk about the subjects that have engaged their
attention, and in your case these have been the emptiest
trifles.   Do you expect that a man like your husband would
care to discuss the latest fashion in bonnets, or the dress
worn by Lady Southdown at the County Hunt Ball, or the
newest scandal set afloat by malicious gossips, or the details
of the last or the coming lawn tennis tournament? Unquestion-
ably not.   Your husband's strong and cultivated intellect cannot feed upon such husks.   Of this, indeed, you are perfectly
well aware, for you know what topics interested him in the
happy times you profess to regret.

" No ; the truth is, you are no longer able to exchange
ideas with him, because, having given up study and reflection,
you have now-a-days no ideas to exchange.   How can you
talk with him about books, when you never read any ?   Or
about pictures, when you have ceased to sketch and paint ?

Or even about your children and the development of their
character, when you have handed them over to the charge
of an ignorant nursemaid? You have always been so occupied
with inutilities that you have neglected necessary things; and,
until to-day, have never found time to discover that you are
unhappy. Your life has been spent in a feverish activity,
which has had no result. Foolish woman! Ignoring duty,
you have lost happiness."

Saddened by these just and wholesome self-reproaches, Mrs.
Mortimer rose from her lounge, and went upstairs to her children's bedroom. Baby Frank was not lying comfortably; she
raised him in her arms while she adjusted his pillow, and as she
replaced him, pressed a kiss on his forehead. "Good night,
nurse," whispered the child, half asleep. The words went like a
knife to Mrs. Mortimer's bosom. Why did he not say "Mamma?"

Next morning, to the surprise of nurse and the children, she
appeared in the nursery, assisted in washing and dressing them,
chatted and played with them. At first, as she observed with
pain, they were under some restraint, as from the presence of a
stranger; but gradually they renewed their confidence, and
revealed points of character which their mother, a woman of
more than ordinary capacity when she chose to exert it, regarded
with apprehension. She saw that Clara was growing up self-
willed, capricious, vain of her personal appearance, and with all
the airs of a coquette at seven years of age. While George was
rough, ill-mannered, and, she feared, untruthful, besides being
inclined to quarrel with his sister at the slightest provocation.
It was evident that they needed firm and intelligent, though
affectionate, control; a mother's control, of which she had
thoughtlessly deprived them.

In the course of the morning she selected some of her children's left-off clothes, which she thought might fit, or be made to fit, the children of Mrs. Johnson, the virago of Well Lane; and dressing herself in a simple morning costume, she directed her steps towards that unlovely neighbourhood.   On entering Mrs. Johnson's room she found there the same dirt and disorder as on the preceding day; but Mrs. Johnson herself was in a less excited condition.   She expressed her gratitude for Mrs. Mortimer's generosity, and was on the point of decorating her children in what she called "their fine new clothes," when that lady interrupted her,—

"But, first, you must wash them, and comb their hair, my good woman, or they will not do justice to their frocks, I assure you."

Water was brought, and a ragged towel; after a long search, a comb with some of its teeth out was discovered on a shelf above the fire-place.   With these appliances the little Johnsons were soon restored to some degree of cleanliness, and even neatness; and proved to be very pretty children, of whom any parents might have been proud.   When they were arrayed in the cast-off plumes of the Mortimers they looked remarkably well, and were evidently much satisfied with their appearance.

" But the elder girl's frock is too long, and wants a tuck in it. In the other's skirt I see a pleat is loose.   Have you a needle and thread to put them to rights ? "

"Oh, ma'am, they will do beautifully as they are ! "

"No ; you must repair them properly by this time to-morrow, or I shall not help you further.   Believe me, Mrs. Johnson, your husband will be quite pleased when his children look tidy and well-cared-for ; and I think he will not go so often to the 'Spread Eagle.'"

Mrs. Johnson shook her head. She had no faith in her husband's amendment, because she had never really tried to bring it about.

After a brief conversation, Mrs. Mortimer took her leave, and returned home. That day, at dinner, she related her adventure to her husband. "Yes," he said, with a sigh, "it is the same in all classes of Society; the husband is so often driven from his home by the faults or follies of his wife." (A good many women would say, perhaps, that many wives are driven by the faults or follies of their husbands!) "If you can reconcile husband and wife, my dear Maud, you will be doing a good work, and if I can assist you I shall do so very gladly."

He sat longer than had lately been his custom, and while playing with his daughter, he asked his wife when she intended to send her to school or to engage a governess for her. "She is seven years old," he remarked, "and it is time that she learned to read."

"I shall begin with her myself to-morrow," replied Mrs. Mortimer, "and with George also, for he is now five years old."

"What! you, Maud?" exclaimed Mr. Mortimer, not less pleased than surprised. "But how will you find time, with all your visits and réunions, your bazaars, and other lady-like amusements?"

Had Mrs. Mortimer spoken frankly, she would have acknowledged that she was growing weary of her incessant round of gaieties; but she evaded the confession by saying that she had no engagements that week.

Her husband smiled, stooped, and kissed her forehead, and retired to his library.

Next day, after breakfast, Mrs. Mortimer began her tuition.

She found the task very troublesome, for the children were
wholly unused to restraint, and fidgetted and trifled until she
felt disposed to throw away her book, and send them off to
play. She summoned up, however, all her patience and resolution, and was rewarded by fixing, at last, the attention of her
two little pupils, and making some progress with them. Afterwards she made a tour of inspection from attic to basement,
and detected many irregularities and disorders due to the
absence of a mistress's watchful eye. " This, and this, and
this," she said to herself, "must be reformed."

While crossing the hall she heard the door-bell ring, and hastily
stepped aside into an ante-room, which commanded a view of the
street door. A young man was admitted, who asked to see Mr.
Mortimer ; but on being informed by the footman that his master
was not at home, was on the point of retiring, with evident looks
of disappointment, when Mrs. Mortimer came forward, and
inquired his business. Removing his hat, he explained that he
wished to obtain Mr. Mortimer's opinion on a memorial he was
to lay, next day, before a Government Commission ; but that,
as Mr. Mortimer was unfortunately out, he would take it to Mr.
Hartmere, the only other gentleman in the town with sufficient
scientific knowledge. Mrs. Mortimer assured him that her
husband would be home to dinner, and thought she could
promise that he would read his manuscript that evening, and
send him a written opinion.

The young man gladly left his manuscript in Mrs. Mortimer's
hands, thanked her warmly, and withdrew ; while she passed
on to her husband's study, where she found the table littered
with books and periodicals deep in dust.

" Oh, it was not like this," she murmured, "in our happier

days ! He studied assiduously then, and kept abreast of the research and discovery of the time ; but now he seems to have lost his interest in books. That dreadful club ! But no ! let me be honest—the club is less to blame than I am.''

*   *   *   *   *

In the evening, after the children had gone upstairs, Mr. Mortimer was astonished to see his wife enter the library, and seat herself in one of the *fauteuils*, as if she intended to be a fixture. She was dressed in white, and for a moment her husband mistook her object. " I beg your pardon, Maud,'' he exclaimed, " I had forgotten I had to take you to some- body's ball."

" No, I am not going to any ball this evening. I want to mend up a few clothes for the poor woman I told you of ; she is too clumsy to handle a needle properly. If I shall not dis- turb you I will do my work in here, and stitch beside you, without making *any* noise, while you run over the pamphlet left by a young man this morning for your examination. I ventured to promise, George, that you would not disappoint him."

" What ? am I to work this evening ? Well, so be it, since you set me a good example." And he took the manuscript, which he began to read with care, taking notes as he proceeded.

Warm were the thanks which the young author bestowed on his critical reader next day. And warm, too, were the thanks which Mrs. Johnson bestowed on Mrs. Mortimer, when that lady appeared with some additional garments for the children and herself. The room looked quite clean and tidy ; for the mother had been afraid lest the " fine new clothes " should be sullied and spoiled, and had set to work with vigour, sweeping, scrubbing, and dusting. It was a welcome surprise to the man Johnson when he returned home ; and that evening he forgot to visit the " Spread Eagle."

      *   *   *   *   *

Weeks passed away, and all was peace and concord within the walls of Redleaf House. As for the room in the dismal yard off Well Lane, it was a miniature Paradise. Mrs. Johnson was indolent by nature, but she was not wanting in intelligence, and she soon learned that it was easier to agree with her husband than to thwart him. She acquired a taste for cleanliness and decorum ; fully appreciated the comforts which she owed to Mrs. Mortimer's generosity; and, in order to ensure their continuance, kept her house in excellent condition, while between her husband and herself more cordial relations were established. Mrs. Mortimer, while befriending this poor woman and her family, did not neglect the claims of her own household. She put an end to the irregularities that always creep up among servants who know their mistress's eye is not upon them. She accepted no more invitations to balls and other entertainments than her husband's social position rendered necessary; spent some of her leisure daily in reading that she might be able to converse with her husband upon literary questions; frequently set up her easel out-of-doors, and painted effective landscapes ; while she delighted her husband after dinner with a sonata of Beethoven or Mozart, and a mazurka or waltz by Chopin. The children were seldom absent from her side ; and while winning their affections, she had contrived to develope their minds and to refine their manners. She conversed with them freely, studied their characters, and felt that the better she

F

understood the more she loved them. She soon taught them to read. Clara was lively and quick of apprehension ; by making her ashamed of her ignorance, her mother stimulated her faculty of application. George discarded his habit of prevarication, and showed a taste for pictures, which his father regarded as a sign that he had inherited his mother's artistic talent. Of baby Frank it is unnecessary to speak.

"Come here, Maud, my love," said Mr. Mortimer, one evening, as he saw her happy face, so fair and serene, looking down on the happy faces of her children, " Come here, and listen to a poet's song, which is just the song I would write to you if Heaven had blessed me with the poet's gift of expression :—

> "'One so fair—none so fair,
>   In thine eyes so true
> Love's most inner heaven bare
>   To the balmiest blue !
>
> One so fair—none so fair,
>   In the skies no star
> Like my star of earth so near—
>   They but shine afar.
>
> One so fair—none so fair,
>   O my bosom guest !
> Love ne'er smiled a happier pair
>   To the bridal-nest.
>
> One so fair—none so fair,
>   Lean on me, sweet wife ;
> Light will be the load we bear,
>   Two hearts in one life.'"

When he had finished reading he drew his wife towards him, and their lips met in a true and tender kiss.

"Ah, George," said Mrs. Mortimer, "I thank God that I saw my folly in time !"

IV.

SOMAL LODGE: A STORY OF THE INDIAN MUTINY.*

YOU know, perhaps, the green lane that turns off to the right, just beyond Crayford Church? It is a lovely lane,—a real English lane,—winding in the cool shade of elm, and ash, and oak, between grassy banks crowned by blooming hedge of hawthorn; and in the summer months the Crayford children resort to it to gather posies of wild flowers in its picturesque recesses. About half way down, the hedge, on the south side, is kept well trimmed and cut rather low, so that the wayfarer catches a glimpse of glowing garden ground, laid out in flower beds of quaint device, and relieved by patches of smooth lawn; and in the rear of this, of a white one-storied cottage, or rather villa, with gabled roof, and in front a low verandah, up the trellis-work of which twine pretty creepers, all very charming and delightful, and conveying the idea that the inmates of the said cottage or villa—it is too large for "a cottage," and too small for "a mansion," and so, I suppose, the builders would call it "a villa"—must be people blessed with that nicest of all endowments, a refined taste. Well, when I was a resident at Crayford, Somal Lodge was occupied by a retired Indian officer, a Major Cameron. "Somal Lodge!

* Adapted from "Le Turban Blanc," of Madame De Witt.

what a strange name !'" said every stranger, whom his Crayford
friends took for a walk down Church Lane; "Somal Lodge!
what could induce the owner to christen his abode by so out-
landish a designation ?" And then, to the stranger making this
obvious and oft-repeated observation, his Crayford friends would
tell the following story :—

"Mamma," said little Ronald Cameron, "there is someone
crying down in the huts yonder. I fear that Nansurah's children
are very hungry."

"I should not wonder," replied his mother, with calm indifference; "rice is dear, and Somal's wages, you know, are
not very good."

"Yes, I know they are not good, and yet he and his wife
have to keep six children upon them," rejoined Ronald, with an
energy which the hot climate of India had not yet succeeded in
subduing.

He was seven years old. Most English children are sent back
to England at a much earlier age; but he was an only son, and
his parents had been unable to make up their minds to part
with him. In the hot season, however, they had always taken
him to the hills, and by this means had succeeded in keeping
him in excellent health. But it had recently been settled that,
in the following spring, he was to return to England, and reside
for a while at Crayford with his maternal grandfather. His
father feared that he might be attacked by one of the diseases
peculiar to the climate. He was anxious also that he should
receive a proper education, to fit him for his future position, as
an officer and a gentleman. It was impossible to keep a boy
of so active and vigorous a disposition satisfied within the
narrow limits of a bungalow, and he was always on the alert to

seize any opportunity of visiting the native quarters, talking to the Hindu women, and playing with the children. " I do not know," said his mother to her husband, " how Ronald has contrived to learn so much Hindustani, but he manages to make himself understood by everybody. Now *I* can't make out a single word."

"You are not such a chatterer as Ronald, my love," said Captain Cameron, laughing. " The poor boy, you see, has no companions of his own age. If he had one or two sisters, or if there were any boys in the station as old as himself, he would not take so much interest in Nansurah's children."

" I cannot comprehend," said Mrs. Cameron, with an air of disgust, " how he can touch those yellow-skinned brats." And her husband, though he lived among yellow-skinned Sepoys, was of the same opinion ; for at this time the Great Mutiny had not opened the eyes of our countrymen to the danger and unwisdom of their contemptuous treatment of their Indian fellow-subjects, whom they did not scruple to vilify as " niggers."

Ronald, meanwhile, had left the room, and skipping and bounding along the verandah, which is the indispensable accompaniment of an Indian bungalow, soon found his way to the quarters occupied by the native servants and their families. Somal, one of Captain Cameron's servants, was busily engaged at his master's, but his wife, Nansurah, was in her hut, surrounded by her dusky children. Some were crying loudly, others weeping silently, while a little girl, of about the same age as Ronald, stood with large sad eyes fixed on the babe whom her mother held upon her knees.

" What is the matter with Rali?" inquired Ronald, who,

plunging like a bombshell into the interior of the hut, stopped short on observing the sorrow-stricken faces of Nansurah and her eldest daughter.

" He is dead, Sahib," said Nansurah, with a sob; " I carried him to all the holy Brahmans, but they could do nothing for the babe of my bosom,—and now,—he is gone! "

Ronald darted from the hut as impetuously as he had entered it. " I am going for our doctor," he said.

And in a couple of minutes he rushed into the cool, calm, silent bungalow of the medical officer of the station, a grey old Scotchman, who maintained exceptionally close relations with Captain Cameron, being not only a fellow-countryman, but a kinsman.

" Come, uncle," said Ronald, who, however, was not the doctor's nephew, but a cousin very far removed, " come and see Rali, Nansurah's baby, he is dying, or perhaps dead! "

" She has six or seven others, hasn't she?" growled the doctor, " and nothing for them to eat; one more or one less, what does it matter?"

" Oh, uncle! " cried Ronald, with a child's frank indignation; " she loves all of them, and haven't you told me that you were one of a family of fifteen, and that your mother loved all alike? "

" Aye, aye, indeed, the poor blessed woman—I am sure of that; but would you go to compare, my fine brave bairn, a brave and noble-minded Scotch lady, brought up in the light of God's Word, with a poor Hindu woman, who does not know or care whether she has a soul to save?"

Ronald had no mind for any such subtle inquiry. He caught hold of the doctor's coat, and dragged him towards the door, with the simple words, " Poor little Rali is dead or dying, uncle, and you *must* come."

They soon arrived at Nansurah's hut. Her baby, they found, had wakened out of the stupor which she had mistaken for death, to be seized with violent convulsions. Dr. Forbes seized a small pot which was simmering over the scanty fire, and without waiting to drain off the rice that was cooking in it, gave the child an impromptu hot bath. It struggled violently at first, and Nansurah was on the point of tearing the sufferer out of the doctor's hands, when she saw that its rigid limbs gradually relaxed, its contracted features recovered their natural sweetness, its clenched fingers loosened their imaginary grasp, and poor little Rali was saved.

" A hot water bath the moment the convulsion commences," remarked Dr. Forbes, "and you may rescue him from this sort of attack twice or even three times," he added, between his teeth, after a rapid examination of the poor little creature, who was by this time sleeping calmly in its mother's arms.

A wail of grief rose from the group of half-naked children, who had huddled together in a corner of the hut, terrified by the grey-haired doctor's entrance and the rapidity of his movements. They had just realized the fact that Rali had been bathed in the pot in which their dinner was cooking. Their hope of satisfying their hunger died away, for the rice was spoiled, and they had no other food to fall back upon.

. The doctor had quitted the hut, and Ronald was about to follow him, but paused for a minute to take a last look at the baby, and to listen to the blessings which the poor mother invoked upon his head. Turning towards the other children, he exclaimed, in Hindustani, and in a tone of authority, " You

will wake Rali !"   The eldest stepped forward ; she was of the
same age as Ronald, but the difference was very great between
his sturdy limbs, rosy cheeks, white forehead, and mass of
auburn curls, and the copper-coloured complexion, black hair,
and frail, meagre body of the poor Hindu girl.   There was
only one point of resemblance between them : both had eyes as
black as jet.   "He has stolen those eyes from some Hindu
child," his mother would sometimes exclaim, with a laugh ;
" His father's eyes are grey, and in my family everybody has
hazel eyes like mine."

Ronald fixed his black eyes on those of Nana.

"Why do you cry?" said he, very kindly.

"Because we have nothing to eat, now that the Sahib doctor
has bathed poor Rali in the rice water."

" Eh, now, that is true ; we must throw it away, of course.   I
am sorry I cannot bring you my own dinner, Nana, for you
would not eat it ; but I will get you some money."

And at full speed Ronald returned to his father's bungalow,
broke like a tornado into his little room, and searched in the
pockets of all his trousers, until he found the purse which contained his private treasure.   It was not a large sum ; but
Nansurah's wants were not many.   In the time that it has taken
us to describe his movements, he was back again in the hut,
holding in his hand the price of five or six measures of rice.

" Here, Nana, here is money enough to buy you a meal, and
is Rali all right now, Nansurah?" he inquired, bending over
the sleeping infant.

With a glance of the most fervent gratitude, the poor Hindu
answered, " You have saved his life !" and she stooped to kiss
the little boy's hand.

Ronald blushed, drew back his hand, and took to flight.

Two days afterwards, poor little Rali died, in the agonies of another convulsive fit, and Ronald mourned for him almost as much as his mother and Nana ; Somal, his father, did not shed a tear ; still and stern, he contemplated the corpse of his child, and the sad countenances of his wife and daughter ; there he stood like a statue, except when an involuntary quiver of the lips revealed the force of his emotions. At length, he turned his eyes upon Ronald, who had fallen on his knees, with his head in his hands, silent in the midst of the children's despairing cries. In a minute or two, Ronald rose. "I have prayed God to preserve your other children to you, Somal," said he, his keen eye detecting under the apparent indifference of the Hindu father how cruelly he suffered.

Somal did not answer, but his eyes wore a gentle and grateful expression. Noiselessly Ronald left the hut, and the Hindu seated himself by his wife's side.

It cannot be said that Captain and Mrs. Cameron showed any special interest in their little son's amusements. The lonely child was left to invent occupations, and games, and objects for himself. His lessons were short, and not very difficult. His mother was indulgent to the extreme ; only his father, accustomed to military discipline, sometimes drew the rein tightly, and always insisted that he should be at home and dressed in good time for dinner. On this occasion, Ronald knew that he was late, and was hurriedly washing his hands and brushing his entangled locks, when he heard his mother, in the adjoining bedroom, say to her husband, "Is it so, Douglas ?"

" Yes ; the men have certainly a discontented air. Ominous reports are circulating, and the Colonel's despatches bring indifferent news from Delhi as well as from Lucknow."

" What will become of us in this isolated station," murmured Mrs. Cameron, " if there should be any outbreak ? "

"God knows," replied Captain Cameron, continuing his toilette with his accustomed composure.

Ronald was petrified. The Sepoys discontented ! An outbreak ! What meant his mother's perturbed air, and the resolute, almost menacing tone adopted by his father ? The Sepoys, or native soldiers, had always seemed to Ronald so many obedient machines, who obeyed orders with instantaneous celerity and the utmost impassability. He had never ventured, however, into their cantonment, though a familiar guest among the huts of his father's servants.

Nearly all the Sepoys were Muhammadans, whereas Somal, Nansurah, and all the servants belonged to the old Hindu faith. Consequently, between them and the Muhammadan soldiers a great gulf was fixed.

At this epoch the Anglo-Indian officers were almost everywhere on the alert. Right bravely they faced the danger which they suspected to be at hand, endeavouring to re-assure their men by displaying unlimited confidence in them ; often sending down their beds to the parade ground, and sleeping there unarmed in front of the men's huts, the armed sentinels marching to and fro beside them. And at times, indeed, when talking to the men—men who had never before been otherwise than docile and respectful—it seemed impossible to doubt their protestations of loyalty, their declarations even of detestation of the conduct of the regiments which had mutinied, and their professions of eagerness to be led against the common enemy. And yet a change had come over them which could not but be observed—a certain sullenness of manner, a look as of suspicion that they were suspected, which the officers in vain endeavoured by their own appearance of confidence to ignore.

At Fyzarabad, however, the officers for the most part implicitly believed in the general loyalty of their men.   When his wife spoke of danger, even Captain Cameron, who at first had shown some apprehension, replied—

"That the Sepoys, or some of them, are grumbling, is true. We shall have to shoot one or two to restore discipline, and then we shall go on all right again.   In the large military cantonments things, perhaps, will assume a graver aspect, but here the regiment is loyal, and our Colonel has a firm hand."

But the fires were burning beneath the embers; and everybody knows how they broke out one day, all suddenly, and spread like a train of powder from point to point, until the greater part of India was involved in strife and bloodshed.   The beginning was at Meerut, on the 10th of May, when the 3rd (native) cavalry revolted, and was followed by the two infantry regiments (the 11th and 20th) then in cantonments.   Europeans were remorselessly butchered—officers, soldiers, and civilians. A large British force was stationed at Meerut, and had it been promptly and vigorously utilised by General Hewit, the chief in command, little doubt exists but that the mutineers might have been severely punished, and the insurrection arrested.   But he did nothing.   The night of the 10th and 11th of May was an awful night at Meerut.   The rebel Sepoys set fire to the European quarters, and massacred innocent women and children; yet the British Commander made no effort to check their cruel wrath. Nor when, two thousand strong, they marched out on their way to Delhi, did he attempt to intercept or pursue them.   To this extraordinary and almost criminal indecision or supineness the historian is compelled to attribute in no small degree the dis-aster which afterwards shook to its foundations the British Power in India.

The mutineers reached the sacred city of Delhi early on the morning of the 12th. Gathering beneath the windows of the old King's palace, they loudly demanded admittance, calling upon him to help them, and proclaiming that they had killed the English at Meerut, and had " come to fight for the faith."

They were welcomed with open arms by the Sepoy regiments of "the sacred city," and the work of murder and destruction began afresh. So full of uproar and confusion was the scene, that the old King was bewildered, terror-stricken. " The mur-derers, with their blood-stained swords in their hands, went about boasting of their crimes, and calling upon others to follow their example. The courtyards and corridors of the palace were swarming with the mutineers of the 3rd cavalry and of the 38th, and soon the Meerut regiments began to swell the danger-ous crowd, whilst an excited Muhammadan rabble mingled with the Sepoys and the palace guards. The troopers stabled their horses in the courts of the palace. The footmen, weary with the long night march, turned the hall of audience into a barrack and littered down on the floor. Guards were posted all about the palace, and the wretched helpless King found that his royal dwelling-house was in military occupation."

Swiftly perceiving the danger that menaced the safety of the Empire, two gallant English officers, Lieutenants Willoughby and Forrest, at the imminent risk of their lives, blew up the great Delhi magazine, thus depriving the mutineers of the abun-dant resource they would otherwise have found in its vast stores

of military *matériel*.   Then those Europeans, with their wives
and children, who had escaped the blood-rage of the revolted
Sepoys, hastened from Delhi as best they could ; and the
mutineers held undisputed possession of the imperial city,
replaced the old and infirm descendant of the Mughals on the
throne from which he had been deposed, and boasted that the
British *raj* was at an end.

* * * * *

The events that had taken place at Meerut and Delhi were
known with wonderful celerity to the Sepoys at Fyzarabad, who
at once prepared to follow the evil example of their comrades.

It was a hot night in May—so hot that every bungalow in
the compound had its windows open to admit whatever fresh
air the light night-breeze might set astir—when a watcher, if
such there had been, on the high grounds above, might have
seen some black shadows issuing silently from the Sepoy lines.
No alarm was given by the sentries ; not a dog barked, so well
and carefully had the mutineers laid their plans.   Gradually
the officers' houses were surrounded, while their Hindu servants
lay shivering in their huts ; for belonging to the lowest castes of
Hindu social life, they looked up with terror, almost with awe,
to the bold Sepoys who had undertaken the deliverance of their
country, and promised to revenge upon the English the supposed
insults they had offered to their ancient faith.

Meanwhile, through the still and solemn night, a shadow,
which was not that of a Sepoy, crept slowly to the platform on
which Major Cameron's bungalow was situated.   A man stole
along the balustrade, scarcely visible in the shade cast by
the raised jalousies.   He advanced stealthily, and with the

utmost caution; now and then a moonbeam fell on his white turban; again he passed into the shade, and remained motionless. Suddenly, a score of Sepoys scaled the small verandah, and while some burst open the doors, others forced their way in through the open windows.

Ten minutes later, and the silence of death brooded over the desolated house. Mrs. Cameron, happily for her, had fallen by the first shot fired; Captain Cameron defended himself with his revolver for an instant, and then, riddled with bullets, fell dead on his wife's corpse. They had been surprised in their sleep; and the agonized mother had time only to cry "Ronald" before she was stricken down.

After hastily pillaging the house; thrusting a dagger into the bed of the "little Sahib," which, however, was empty; and shooting Mrs. Cameron's old and faithful nurse, who had been with her since her childhood; the Sepoys passed on to attack another officer's residence. Their *coups de main*, however, were not all so successful. Colonel Forbes was on guard with his aides-de-camp; he had barricaded his bungalow, and resisted the fierce attacks of the mutineers with immoveable persistency. His wife, standing behind him, loaded the rifles, and handed them to the little band of defenders with unshaken composure, turning occasionally to cast a sorrowful glance at her young daughters, who, trembling with terror, crouched in a corner of the room. "Courage, Maria; courage, Ada," she cried, "God is with us!"

While the work of death went on apace through the station; while the crack of musketry, and the whirr of bullets, the yells of the infuriated Sepoys, and the stern shouts of the English officers, combined in an awful discordant chorus; while the moonlight was eclipsed by the appalling glare of the burning bungalows, as, one after the other, their thatched roofs shot into flame ; Somal, with a child in his arms, rushed into his cabin, seized a pot of the paint which he used to dye his body, and quickly painted Ronald as tawny as himself. The boy's auburn curls fell beneath the rapid movements of Nansurah's scissors ; a white turban was placed on his head ; the little English boy had disappeared, and Nana herself could not have penetrated the disguise. He himself was too sleepy and confused to speak. Snatched from his bed by Somal at the first indication of the Sepoys' attack, he had not heard his mother's despairing cry, and had been rapidly conveyed through the deserted offices to the rear of the house, where Somal had wrapped him up in a piece of canvas, that he might look like a bundle containing his share of the plunder. The poor boy felt as if in a wild, hurried dream. He had resisted for a moment when the native covered him with the canvas ; but the latter made a gesture commanding silence, and he had instantly obeyed.

Without uttering a word, Somal again caught up the child. Nansurah put in a bag some handfuls of rice, and a gourd of fresh water ; and husband and wife exchanging a mute farewell, the Hindu, with his living burden, plunged anew into the shadows.

The loud demoniacal yells, the dropping shots, the hissing flames, awakened Ronald completely, and he made a violent effort to escape from the arms which held him.

" Where are you taking me, Somal ?" he said, in a low voice ; " I want to go to mamma."

A dreadful outcry, in a bungalow which they passed, fright-

ened him into silence.   He could see the Sepoys, in the midst
of the flames, brandishing their bayonets, and women
struggling in their ferocious grasp.   Trembling all over, he laid
his head on Somal's shoulder, and wept silently.

The Hindu moved onward, with a step swift and sure ; and
had got well into the forest before the crests of the tallest trees
had been touched with golden glory by the rays of morn ;
under their close-woven canopy the path wound through fes-
toons of parasites and climbing plants, in a kind of green
twilight.   Somal had reflected that it was imperative he should
push forward as rapidly as possible at the very beginning of the
outbreak, while the Sepoys were engaged in their bloody and
destructive work.   He calculated that afterwards they would be
delayed for some time by their love of plunder ; and that the
day would be far advanced before they dispersed in pursuit of
fugitives.   For some hours, at least, the forest would offer a
secure asylum, and Somal felt that he must take a brief rest.
He deposited Ronald by the side of a small, but crystal spring,
and proceeded to quench his thirst.   The boy in his turn crept
to the grassy edge, and as he stooped, saw in the clear mirror
before him, his yellow countenance, his white turban, and his
robe of dark blue.   He did not recognize himself, and in
strange confusion of mind, cried out :

"You have deceived yourself, and taken one of your own
children in my place, Somal !"

Recovering himself immediately, and smiling at his absurd
"bull," he continued :

"But no, I see it now, you have disguised me cleverly !
Why, mamma would not know me !   Oh, Somal, where is
mamma ?   Why did you not wake her when you woke me ?"

The truth could not long be hidden, and indeed, it was desirable that Ronald should know it, in order to understand the nature of the peril he had escaped, and be the better prepared to confront those which still lay in his path.

"The mother of the little Sahib sleeps so soundly, that Somal could never have wakened her," answered the Hindu, in a grave voice.

Ronald leaped to his feet.

"Mamma! papa!" and he shouted until he was hoarse.

"Are they dead? Tell me, have the Sepoys killed them?"

Somal bent his head, without speaking.

"Oh, if I were only tall, like a man," cried Ronald, and the spirit of his race flashed in his eyes. "If I were but a man, I would go back to the station, and dash into the midst of the villains and avenge my parents! I *would* avenge them."

The poor boy's voice was drowned in tears, and he threw himself on the ground, concealing his face in his hands. Somal stood motionless; he wept also, but it was silently, with the quiet patience of the Hindu. What had become of Nansurah and her children, left without a protector in the midst of a horde of ruffians?

Ronald was still weeping, when the Hindu arose, put his finger on his lips, and then, drawing from his bag a handful of rice, offered it to Ronald, making him a sign to eat of it. The child obeyed mechanically. A vague trembling of the leaves reached his ears, but without waking in him any fear of danger. Somal, however, while appearing to eat, listened attentively, and suddenly, at the end of a leafy glade, three Sepoys made their appearance, with their uniform disordered, their turbans scorched and blackened by the flames, and their flashing eyes and fierce

G

countenances only too plainly showing that they had taken part in the bloody strife. They conversed with one another in loud tones, not observing Somal and his little companion, who were half-hidden in the thicket near the spring.

"The Captain—his sword—his pistols" were the words they dropped as they came near their retreat.

Ronald at once recognized them as soldiers of his father's company, and he perceived that they were carrying off a valuable jewelled sword, which had been presented to his father for some deed of valour, and a pair of silver-mounted pistols, which his father always kept by the side of his bed. A flush of emotion crossed his face, but Somal made him an almost imperceptible sign to keep still. The Sepoys, as they passed, exchanged a brief greeting with Somal, but took no notice of the yellow-skinned boy with the white turban, seated on the bank of the little stream.

"Oh, if I were but a man !" exclaimed Ronald, when the murderers had gone by.

" If my little Sahib would live to be a man," said the Hindu, "he must be very cautious and silent now."

"Yes, Somal, I will be," and they resumed their journey in a direction opposite to that which had been taken by the Sepoys. But Ronald would not allow Somal to carry him any longer, and trotted on by his side with courageous perseverance. It was a long and wearisome journey. For twelve days the travellers continued to advance, sometimes through the glades of the woods, sometimes across wide plains, generally resting by day and making their marches by night. Nansurah's rice was soon exhausted, and as neither had any money, they lived on the fruit they picked in woods, or on the handfuls of rice they begged from charitable women in the villages they passed through. India, at this time, was covered with mendicants, who sought to hide, under their rags and tatters, the white skin and fair hair of the English race, but were too often recognized and murdered. Those blue eyes, transmitted from our Norse forefathers, cost the lives of their possessors. One day Ronald saw a little girl killed, whom a faithful Sepoy was endeavouring to convey to a place of safety. She was disguised like himself, but her bright, azure eyes could not be concealed ; she turned them in alarm towards the villain who insulted her protector, and the glance betrayed her—both she and her bearer were immediately cut down.

As the days passed by, it was with increasing difficulty that our two travellers continued their journey. Ronald never complained ; but the terrible fatigue, and want of sufficient food and sleep, had consumed all his childish strength. His weary limbs and bleeding feet could scarcely support him ; yet he refused to allow Somal to carry him, and it was only when from sheer exhaustion, he fell into an uneasy slumber, that Somal could take him in his arms, and press forward with some degree of rapidity. They, at last, drew near the Ganges, where Somal hoped to fall in with a boat that would convey them to Calcutta. Wandering bodies of Sepoys began to be numerous, and in the villages he heard rumours of British troops driving before them a beaten and dispirited enemy. Ronald had completely succumbed to the fatigue, and was asleep in Somal's arms, when a harsh voice close to his ear, aroused him. " Oh, dog ! you paint the white men's children in order to save them ! " And a blow from the butt end of a musket stretched Somal and his burden on the ground. Instinctively, Ronald uttered in Hindustani, a prayer for mercy. "What!" said the drunken Sepoy, "have I made a mistake?" and he staggered away without molesting them further.

The boy then freed himself from the nerveless arms of the Hindu, who lay with his eyes closed, to all appearance dead. Ronald ran down to the river, filled his gourd with water, and was bathing the forehead and lips of his faithful protector when a boat touched the bank close by him. It was manned by a couple of English officers, who had been sent out to reconnoitre, and was followed by a big barge filled with redcoats—a welcome sight to little Ronald, who ran up to the officers, and exclaimed, "I am Ronald Cameron, son of Captain Cameron. Please help poor Somal; he has brought me all the way from Fyzara-bad, and saved me from the cruel Sepoys; but he has just been wounded, and I cannot get him to open his eyes."

. In spite of his disguise and painted skin, the colour of which, however, was beginning to wear off, the two officers recognized Ronald's nationality, and welcomed him warmly. By their order Somal was carried on board the barge, and Ronald was about to be transferred to their own boat, when he exclaimed, " No, no, let me remain with Somal, who will think me lost if he does not see me on opening his eyes."

Somal opened his eyes, but he did not recognize Ronald. The violent blow which he had received on his head, added to the effect of the heavy fatigue he had undergone, had broken him down, both mentally and physically. He repulsed Ronald, mistaking him for one of his own children, and exclaimed, " I must look after my little Sahib, who wept so much when Rali died."

Ronald wept now, and wept as if his heart would break; but

the English officers insisted on his accompanying them when they saw that his faithful servant was delirious, and having completed their reconnaissance, set out on their return to Calcutta.

The orphan boy was soon in safety in the Governor-General's palace, where he was affectionately received and cared for by Lady Canning. Poor Somal died on the following day; but Lord Canning sent instructions to the authorities at Fyzarabad, where order had been re-established, to provide for the future comfort and support of Nansurah and her children, and publicly to recognize the heroic fidelity of Nansurah's husband.

As for Ronald, his maternal grandfather at Crayford undertook his education, and after a brilliant career at the Crayford Grammar School, he was sent to Woolwich. He passed his examinations with *eclât*, and received a commission in the—— Regiment, which he accompanied in all its migrations, finally serving with it in the Egyptian Campaign. A severe wound at the battle of Tel-el-Kebir compelled him to retire from the profession. Returning to Crayford, he married a young lady to whom he had been attached since his early manhood, and, purchasing a piece of ground in Church Lane, built the pretty and picturesque villa which, in remembrance of the faithful Hindu to whose devotion he owes his. life, he has christened *Somal Lodge.*

V.

THE BEECHES; OR, A STORY OF ADVENTURE.

OF course anybody could have told they were lovers, aye, and "engaged" lovers—the young couple who stood, one beautiful autumn night, a year or two ago, at the garden-gate of Mrs. Durham's pretty house.

Mrs. Durham, the owner of The Beeches, was, let me tell you, well known and highly respected in Crayford. She was the widow of a gentleman farmer, who, ten years before, had broken his neck in the hunting field, leaving her with an only child, a girl of nine, to face the world as best she might. For Mrs. Durham, however, the task was not so difficult as it proves for too many widows, as her husband had left her adequately provided for; but still, an "unprotected female," to adopt a popular phrase, has always a good many obstacles to contend with—false friends, greedy speculators, fortune-hunters, and the like. Over these and others Mrs. Durham's good sense had carried her successfully, and recently her happiness had been crowned by the engagement of her daughter Eva, a beautiful maiden of nineteen summers, to Lieutenant Walter Eyre, of the Royal Navy, second son of Mr. Eyre, of Crayford Manor.

It was Lieutenant Eyre and Eva Durham who were saying good-bye at the garden gate of Mrs. Durham's house on the

night I speak of. They were standing in the shade of a noble
elm, and Walter's arm encircled Eva's waist by right of future
proprietorship. Though they had spent the evening together,
they had still a good deal to say that must be said—as is the
way with their kind ; for I have known a pair of lovers spend
the whole day in each other's company, and yet, when the time
for parting came, to be as earnestly engaged in the closest and
most important conversation as if they had not met for years.
Well, there was some excuse for Eva and her gallant lover,
inasmuch as he was under orders to join his ship at Portsmouth
on the following evening ; and consequently had to leave early
in the morning, before his pretty Eva's dark blue eyes would
have opened on the light of day. They were taking leave of each
other, therefore, with the knowledge that some months would
elapse before they met again ; and in such circumstances, is it to
be wondered at that they took a long time to say "Farewell ?"

"Farewell, a word that must be and hath been"—always a
painful word—the painfullest, perhaps, in our language—yet
on this occasion, and for this fortunate young man and maiden,
robbed of a good deal of its painfulness by the knowledge that,
subject to the ordinary chances and changes of mortal life, in a
few months they would meet again ; that their true pure love
had run its course without impediment ; that their betrothal had
taken place with the warm approval of both their families ; and
that on the Lieutenant's return they were to be married. The
tears, nevertheless, gathered thickly in Eva's sweet dark eyes,
supplying Walter with pleasant occupation in kissing them
away ; and it was with a tremulous voice she begged him to
write at every opportunity, and dwelt on the dangers always
awaiting those who go down to the sea in ships.

"Is the 'Calypso' a safe vessel, Walter?"

"She is one of the ships of Her Majesty's Navy," replied the Lieutenant, laughing, "and therefore we are bound to suppose she is everything that she should be. And I must confess that I don't think she'll turn over like a turtle, or shed her masts as a crab sheds its legs."

"Do you like your captain?"

"Captain Digby?—oh, very much! he's jolly—very jolly—keeps strict discipline, but knows when the reins will bear loosing; he is respected and beloved by both officers and men. Oh! we shall have a splendid voyage, Eva."

"You will think me foolish, Walter, but I have a foreboding—"

"My love, don't have forebodings, they are disagreeable, and worth nothing. Never prophesy unless you know; or, if you don't know, and yet *will* prophesy, prophesy good things. They are much nicer to anticipate than evil things."

"There! I was certain you would laugh at me."

"No, no, not at *you*, my darling."

"And yet I cannot overcome the feeling that some misfortune is to befall you on this voyage. God grant that it may not be so, for—for—you are so very, very dear to—me—that—"

"Dearest Eva, this is fanciful, and quite unlike the usual excellent good sense of the future Mrs. Eyre. Let us put our trust in the mercy of Heaven, dearest. And oh, my darling, have I not the knowledge of your devoted love to shield, and encourage, and sustain me? What a thrice fortunate man I am in having won the heart of the best and brightest girl in England! But now, dearest Eva, one more kiss and—Good-bye."

"Good-bye, dearest, dearest Walter! May God bless and preserve you, and bring you back in safety to your own Eva!"

The lovers parted; and next morning Lieutenant Eyre was on his way to Portsmouth. On the following day his ship set sail.

    *   *   *   *   *

Their course, as far as Kingston, in Jamaica, was unmarked by any incident, and Lieutenant Eyre, in his letters to Eva, did not fail to tease her about her forebodings—everything, he said, was as dull as ditch-water; and one might as well look for a diamond in an oyster, as for an adventure to break the monotony of their daily lives. Soon after their arrival, however, they were despatched on a mission which promised a little excitement: to search for a pirate vessel which had for some time infested the waters of the Caribbean Sea. On the evening of the 26th of August, the "Calypso" lay becalmed, "like a painted ship upon a painted ocean," off the Colorados rocks; when, about eight o'clock, a slight westerly breeze arose, and all sails were spread. It was a beautiful sight: the neighbouring shore, rich in tropical vegetation, glowed with colour; the waves, stirred with a light rippling motion, reflected as in a mirror, the golden azure of the serene heavens. In about an hour, however, the wind shifted suddenly to the south, and a small dark cloud, "no bigger than a man's hand," became visible above the horizon. The Captain recognized at once this omen of coming tempest, and instantly ordering all hands on deck, took in every stitch of canvas, and made his corvette as snug and taut as possible, in the hope of riding out the gale securely.

Longer and darker waxed the cloud: for a few seconds a deadly hush brooded over the sea; and then, in the distance, could be heard a roar and a rush, like that of pealing thunder, which rapidly drew nearer, and nearer, and nearer, while all around,

the blue waters, which but just now had slumbered like a moun-
tain tarn on a summer afternoon, heaved and swelled in masses of
creamy foam before the dense black wall that bore down upon
the "Calypso." The air quaked with a din, like that of the shock
of contending armies. The gale shrieked and screamed, as it
tore on its headlong way through the convulsed atmosphere.
Hitherto, the corvette had rocked gently on the rippling waves,
but, all at once, the fury of the billows fell upon her, and the
hurricane caught her in its tremendous grasp. "Stand by
to cut away the masts!" cried Lieutenant Eyre, for it was his
watch. Too late! Before those of the crew and officers who
were below could rush upon deck, the ship was on her broad-
side, and in a few seconds heeled right over, and began to
sink fast.

For a moment, Lieutenant Eyre caught a glimpse of his comrades struggling for life in that "hell of waters." Then he
struck out vigorously to get clear of the vortex created by the
sinking vessel; found something floating, and clutching at it,
secured one oar and then another. By these means he kept
himself up until the cyclone had swept past and spent its fury,
and the sea subsided into as profound a calm, as if no wind
had vexed its surface since the first days of Creation.

Looking anxiously around to see if any of the officers and
crew had escaped, the Lieutenant, to his great joy, heard the
voice of Captain Digby, inquiring if any one were near. With
six of his men, he was clinging to a boat which had floated up
clear of the wreck. When she was first seen, so many had
hastened to take advantage of this chance of security, that they
capsized her; and some twenty-four men and officers clung to
her desperately, most of them across her keel, so that they had

rendered her useless, except as a float. Captain Digby ordered them all to quit their positions, that she might be righted. A couple of seamen were then placed in her to bale out the water with their hats, while the rest of the survivors supported themselves by hanging round the gun-wales until she was light enough to carry them. But just as they began to bale, one of the men, with staring eyes and pallid countenance, declared that he saw the fin of a shark, and in the terror of falling victims to the monster, the men forgot the restraints of discipline and the dictates of prudence. They struggled violently to get into the boat, and again capsized it.

Lieutenant Eyre now interfered, to restore order, exhibiting a coolness which restored the courage of his men; the boat was righted, the balers were set to work, while the men, acting on their captain's instructions, splashed the water with their legs to keep the enemy at a distance. After almost superhuman exertions, the boat was put into a condition to hold her crew; morning broke with gleams of gold and azure over the shining sea. All promised well, and the castaways began to entertain hopes of safety, when again arose the alarming cry of "A shark! a shark!" and at least fifteen of these terrible foes swept in upon them. For the third time, the men, in a panic of terror, overturned the boat; but patient, and calm, and resolute, Lieutenant Eyre recalled them to their obedience, and the habits of discipline prevailed over the fear of a terrible death.

The boat was once more righted, and the balers resumed their arduous task; while white faces hung outside the gun-wale; and the sharks swam to and fro, at first apparently for no other purpose than amusement. But a sudden cry of agony proclaimed that one

of the creatures had seized a victim; and the men knew only too well
that blood having once been tasted, escape became impossible.
Still the Lieutenant, whose thoughts ever and anon passed away
from the terrible scene, to the quiet pastoral landscapes of
Crayford, and the home of Eva Durham, encouraged his men,
as he held fast by the stern, to keep steady, and wait in grim
patience until the boat could safely hold them.

Successive shrieks, and the crimsoned waters told, again and
again, a melancholy tale. One after another was torn from his hold,
until, at last, only six remained. Among these was the Captain,
whom a blow on the head had rendered incapable of taking the
command. Forgetting for a moment, or no longer possessing the
strength, to splash, he had a leg snapped off. He seemed all
at once to recover his senses, but with the composure of a true
hero, uttered not a groan—lest he should frighten the survivors,
who were ignorant of what had happened—until the cruel jaws
seized the other limb, when, with a cry unconsciously wrung
from him by the shock, he relaxed his hold. Two of the
men promptly caught him in their arms, and lifted his
mutilated body into the boat. His generous courage prevailed
over his physical sufferings, and, raising himself, as his life-
blood ebbed rapidly away, he called to him Lieutenant Eyre,
and bade him, if he escaped, inform the Admiral of all the
circumstances of the calamity that had overtaken them. " Do
justice," he said, "to the patient fortitude and discipline of the
men. I wish I could tell him how nobly. you yourself have
behaved. God grant that you may escape, and live for many
happy years to be a credit to the service !"

He then embraced him warmly, after which he shook each
man by the hand and said " Good-bye," with a word of cheer

for all as long as he could speak. But, exposed to the rays of a burning sun, without food or water, and so fearfully wounded, he sank rapidly, and was probably quite unconscious, when, towards evening, on another alarm from the sharks, a hasty movement among the survivors—in spite of Lieutenant Eyre's entreaties and expostulations—again upset the boat, and he sank beneath the waves.

The Lieutenant was now in command, as indeed he had virtually been from the first. "Come, my men," he exclaimed, "behave like British seamen. There are only five of us now, and the boat will easily hold us if you do not lose your heads." "Aye, aye, Sir," was the hearty response. The boat was righted, and the Lieutenant and his little crew got in. They were sadly exhausted, however, with their long exposure in the water, want of food and drink, and the heat of a Tropical sun : for awhile they leaned over the sides, unable to move—almost powerless to think. The Lieutenant was the first to recover himself : he was nerved to exertion by the recollection of the fair, sweet girl at Crayford, who had given him the precious gift of her virgin love.

Ordering one of the men to continue baling, and tearing up a couple of thwarts, he directed the others to use them as paddles, so as to keep the boat's head to the waves. But about three o'clock in the morning the poor wretches were seized with an attack of delirium, sprang overboard, and perished. The two survivors, Lieutenant Eyre and a seaman named Maclean, were dreadfully shocked by this sad incident. They composed themselves, however, as best they might, and, as the boat was now nearly dry, lay down in her to rest their weary limbs, while the Lieutenant repeated the Lord's

Prayer, and addressed to God an earnest supplication for deliverance. Then Heaven in its mercy sent a deep sleep on the young officer and his companion, to which, in all probability, they owed the preservation of their senses.

The sun was high in the heavens when they awoke—and awoke to a prospect which the Lieutenant, with all his courage, could not contemplate unmoved. They were alone, he and his companion, in a frail boat, under a burning sky; around them the sea swarmed with sharks; and for thirty-six hours they had been without food. The pangs of hunger were not so severe, however, as those of thirst; yet the Lieutenant would not suffer Maclean to drink the salt water, knowing that a temporary relief would be dearly purchased by loss of reason, or, at all events, greater suffering. He endeavoured to keep up the man's spirits and his own by assurances that they were sure to be seen by some passing vessel, and by reciting such passages of poetry as his memory could recall, though at times fatigue got the better of his energetic will, and he fell off into a brief slumber, waking with a start from uneasy dreams, in which he was back again in the bright garden at The Beeches, with Eva Durham by his side.

About eight o'clock in the morning a white speck rose upon the horizon, and the two sufferers gasped out simultaneously, "A sail! A sail!" The flame of Hope shot up anew in each brave heart; officer and seaman clasped each other's hands; with straining eyes they followed the course of the vessel, of which the hull was soon clearly visible. Thank God—she was bearing down upon them! "Thank God," said the Lieutenant to himself, with a devout prayer, "I shall see my Eva again!" Yes, she drew nearer, and still nearer; she was within half-a-mile! But why that sudden change of countenance, that look of blank despair, such as the human face assumes when all is lost, and life no longer affords ground for hope? Alas! she has tacked, and is standing away in a contrary direction. They wave their handkerchiefs; they strain their hoarse voices in a frenzied shout. But she has not noticed them, and continues to sail away—away.

Then a voice seemed to whisper to Lieutenant Eyre that in the receding vessel lay his only chance of salvation. He must make a desperate effort—yes, for the sake of Eva, his betrothed —he must swim after the ship while she was yet in sight. He was a fine swimmer, and gifted by nature with rare physical strength; but then neither strength nor skill could avail against those monsters of the deep which had been the destruction of so many lives. There was, however, no other resource. Every hour would still further exhaust his energies: to remain was certain death, for hunger and thirst would soon claim their victims. He said some farewell words to Maclean, and begged of him, if he saw a shark in pursuit, not to let him know: shook hands, offered a brief prayer to the Almighty Father, commending himself to His guidance, and plunged into the waves.

Maclean was at first desirous of joining him, but his officer saw that he was too feeble, and that the attempt would prove fatal to his own hopes of success. So the poor fellow was left to his solitude, while Eyre, aware that he was making a last effort for life and happiness, breasted the waves with almost superhuman energy, splashing as he went to scare away the sharks, and shouting in order to attract the attention of the crew of the departing vessel. For a while they made no sign; so that when he had swam about two-thirds of the distance, his heart sank, his strength gave way, and he was on the point of resigning himself to float motionless until some shark terminated his sufferings, when he saw a sailor looking out over the ship's bulwarks. He waved his arms—he raised his body in the water—he was seen ! The ship hove to ; a boat was lowered; and in a few minutes he was in safety. He had just strength enough left to tell his wonderful story, and to direct his kind rescuers to the succour of Maclean, before he became delirious.

Care and attention, however, with the aid of a strong constitution, brought him round, though he was in a very feeble condition when he arrived at Kingston, and some weeks elapsed before he could sail for England. At Crayford his recovery was rapid, and, in the early spring, Eva Durham redeemed her promise, and became Mrs. Eyre. She and her husband have taken up their residence at The Beeches, as Mrs. Durham shrank from parting entirely with her only child ; and the gallant officer is, of course, one of the chief "lions" and glories of Crayford. Eva considers that her foreboding of evil was amply justified by the event; but the Lieutenant always shows a disinclination to recall the events of the terrible day and night spent under such appalling circumstances, or to refer to the long and arduous effort which saved the lives of himself and his companion. There are some extremes of suffering which the mind does wisely to forget.

VI

CROSSWAYS COTTAGE: A STORY OF VAULTING AMBITION.

THE high road from Crayford to Winsham is crossed, about a mile from the former town, by the road from Hartington to Spilsbury. At their point of junction, on the right hand side of the Winsham Road, stands a quaint old cottage, built of timber and mortar, with a high thatched gable roof, and a rustic porch, which, in the early summer, blooms with monthly roses and honeysuckles. Beside it is a long low shed, with wide open door, and lattice window, which is used as a smithy. Crossways Cottage, as it is called, is the residence of John Fenner, the blacksmith—a short sturdy man, with arms like those of a Hercules, grizzled hair, and honest furrowed countenance, whose forehead is knit into a hundred wrinkles by dint, no doubt, of many years' contemplation of the sparks elicited from the red hot iron by his energetic blows. John Fenner is very proud of his cottage and his smithy; and he has some reason for his pride. His cottage forms so quaintly picturesque an object, that great artists have transferred it to their canvas, while his smithy is famous through all the country-side, and commands the patronage of everybody in Crayford or Winsham, Hartington or Spilsbury, who has a horse to be

H

shod, or a cart wheel to be new tired ; nor is there a farmer for miles around who would think, if he has smith's work to be done, of going anywhere else than to John Fenner's smithy at the Crossways !

From father to son, for many years, perhaps for many generations, the Fenners had been smiths. I have no doubt that a Fenner rivetted the coat-of-mail of John of Gaunt, shod the horse of Richard III., and sharpened the sword of Cavalier or Puritan in the stormy years of the Civil War. They regarded the vocation of a smith as one of special honour and surpassing importance ; and each succeeding Fenner endeavoured to surpass, or at all events equal, his father, his grandfather, and his great-grandfather. From his infancy the eldest son was solemnly destined to be a smith—dedicated, as it were, to Vulcan—just as the younger son of an English country gentleman was, in the old days, set apart for the Church. To him (thrice happy fellow !) descended the Christian name of John, the gabled cottage with its rose-garlanded porch, and the time-blackened smithy. To him descended the forge and the great bellows, the anvil and the hammers ; and to him descended also the charge of maintaining unsullied the honour of the Fenners.

And you may be sure that he soon learned to appreciate the value and distinction of his inheritance, and that the lord of the manor was not more proud of his lineage and estates. That he should become in his turn John Fenner the elder, instead of John Fenner the younger, was a prospect to which he looked forward with the highest possible sense of its surpassing dignity.

As for the younger Fenners, they lay under the usual disabilities which afflict younger sons ; they did what they could or

would in order to gain a footing in the world; and it is understood that some of them went to sea, and rose to the rank of
boatswain or mate; while others enlisted in the army, and
attained to the sergeant's halberd. Whatever the calling on
which they decided, they always did well in it; for they came
of a good stock, had learned to fear God and honour the Queen,
and were never ashamed of doing their duty. It must be owned,
however, that they did not display any intellectual force or love
of culture; one has never heard of Fenner the poet, Fenner the
artist, or Fenner the physicist. They belonged to the class who
earn their living by the sweat of their brow—the broad-chested,
strong-armed, slow-witted men, who have helped to make
England what she is by their steady perseverance and manly
courage.

From father to son, then, the fortunate world rejoiced in
Fenners, smiths and wheelwrights; and we may add that from
father to son the Fenners, smiths and wheelwrights, were fortunate in their prosperous lives. This might well be the case
with a family whose most precious traditions were those of contentment, truthfulness, temperance, and integrity. They were
never disturbed by aspirations after the unattainable; they were
so satisfied with their own position, that it did not occur to
them to envy that of others. Their sluggish brains took no
interest in political or ethical problems; enough for them to
pay their way, to owe no man anything, and to have something
to spare for the needy wayfarer. Every Sunday, father and
mother, sons and daughters, might be seen on their way to the
old Church at Crayford. There were Churches much nearer
the Crossways, and a little Bethel not two hundred yards off,
but as long as there had been John Fenners, smiths and wheel-

wrights, those John Fenners and all belonging to them had
attended Crayford Church, and this was reason sufficient for
continuing to do so.   No doubt they were behind the age, but
then they were happier than the age, which may be taken as
adequate satisfaction.   The Fenners, men and women, were
round of cheek and plump of limb ; they rose early and went to
bed early, and slept soundly, because their consciences were
untroubled.   Of course they adhered to old English fare ; they
bred their own bacon, grew their own vegetables, and brewed
their own beer—such capital beer that the vicar, and the squire,
and the doctor, if they passed Crossways Cottage, had always
some excuse for looking in upon John Fenner, and joining in a
gossip, which closed invariably with a glass of amber ale as
clear as crystal, and as pure as—but to what shall we venture
to liken the purity of that marvellous and justly celebrated
beverage ?

The John Fenners have been always good business men, with
a keen eye for the things that make business men prosperous,
and in no respect has their shrewdness shown itself more con-
spicuously than in their choice of wives.   Good looks they have
not particularly sought after, and yet, somehow or other, their
wives have been as buxom and attractive as any in or round
about Crayford ; but they have had to be virtuous, well-behaved
young women, brought up by virtuous and well-behaved mothers
—women who could manage a household firmly and yet good
temperedly, with fitting liberality, but without waste.   Such
women are said to be rare, but yet the Fenners always found
them ; first, because they deserved them, and second, because
they were never in a hurry.   If a John Fenner saw a maiden
to his liking, he watched her with slow thoughtful eyes

until he thoroughly understood her character and disposition. Then he began his "courting," which, for the future Mrs. Fenner, was just a kind of apprenticeship to fit her for the discharge of the all-important duties incumbent on the (female) head of Crossways Cottage. This apprenticeship might be prolonged over a year-and-a-half, two years, or even three years, ending, when John Fenner was thoroughly satisfied, with a gold ring and a peal of many bells, and the triumphal escort of the bride by kinsmen and friends to her new and comfortable home.

The life of the Fenners was not distinguished by adventure or incident, and the whole history of the race, from the time of their settlement at Crossways Cottage down to the present, would not furnish material for an ordinary three volume romance.   As day followed day in the same tranquil course, some people, no doubt, would have pronounced it monotonous ; yet there was interest enough and variety enough to occupy the easily satisfied minds of the Fenners.   The farmer brought his cob to be shod, and had a good deal to say about the weather and the crops, bad seasons and American competition ; the carrier stopped for a few minutes to rest his tired horse, and poured out all the news he had collected from the different villages he had passed through ; twice a day the Crayford and Winsham omnibus rattled up with its team of four horses, and "took up" the passengers, who found the Crossways a convenient waiting-station ; the vicar frequently halted to exchange a word or two with John Fenner, and ask after his wife and children ; the gossips of the neighbourhood assembled almost every evening, and leaning against the gateway watched the smith at his work, as if it were something strange and novel which they had never seen before.

Meanwhile, they discoursed in their lethargic rural fashion about such subjects as are dear to the heart of the English peasant, and smoked their pipes with an air of ineffable wisdom.

Florists are well aware that a plant which for many successive years has produced invariably the same kind of leaf and blossom will, all of a sudden, develop something entirely new. A similar "sport" or "freak" of Nature at length took place in the famous Fenner family. Yes; there appeared a wayward and degenerate Fenner, whose ill-wrought disposition refused to accept and act upon the Fenner traditions. It is not easy to explain this untoward phenomenon. Some wise people explained it by reference to the circumstance that he had been christened John Albert, instead of simply and plainly John, like his forefathers; others had always known what would come of John Fenner the elder's folly in marrying "a stranger," that is, a very pretty but rather fantastic damsel who had come down from London to visit a Crayford friend, and had thrown such a glamour over the lord of the Crossways that, neglecting the precautions usually taken by the men of his race, he had married her after a courtship of only three weeks.

However that may be, John Albert Fenner, when he attained to years of puberty, manifested a disposition to break out into new methods and new ways, and was evidently of opinion that things were not necessarily good because they were old. Sad to say, John Fenner the elder, being very much under his wife's influence, was pleased at first with this precocious ambition. Bringing his broad hand down on his son's shoulder, he would exclaim—"Aye, aye, my lad, thou'rt a clever one! Thee'll be the greatest of the Fenners, I can see; aye, greater than your great-grandfather, who shod the horse ridden by Squire Osmond when he won the Spilsbury Steeplechase!" These words only encouraged John Albert's dreamy aspirations, and, soaring high above the little world of Crossways, he longed to display his talents on the wider stage afforded by a large town.

This conviction became so firmly fixed in his mind that one day, when his father boisterously eulogized the young man's abilities, he replied, "I hope to maintain the honour of the family; but I hear that in our trade are many new-fangled things of design and execution which can be learned only in a large town, and from workmen who have been trained at Sheffield. If you be willing to let me go to Spilsbury for a year, I shall pick up——"

John Fenner shook his head. The proposal was so contrary to all the ways of the Fenner family that it revived his conservative principles. Besides, he suspected that his son must have some other design than merely to learn "the new tricks o' the trade" in order to bring them down to Crossways. But John Albert was a clever fellow, and he hammered away at his project with such persistency, and so alarmed his father with the idea of a competitor from Sheffield establishing himself at Crayford, and robbing the Fenners of their county connection, that eventually he yielded. His consent was reluctantly given, and at the last moment would have been recalled but for the influence exercised by his wife.

John Albert set out on the following Monday. His eye was bright and his step elastic, for he believed that he was pressing forward to Fame and Fortune. His father's last words were, "Return as soon as possible;" but John Albert had no intention of hurrying himself. He had heard, or read, that the German workmen, in their years of apprenticeship, wander over the whole country ; and he thought how happy he should be if he could but follow their example.

With a heart elate for any fate, and cherishing the brightest anticipations of future fortune, John Albert went on his way. He intended, when any place particularly pleased him, to obtain employment there ; and then, when he was weary of it, and had put by a sum of money, to seek work in some other town.   He would go to the first smith or wheelwright he saw and ask to be taken on, and to prove his skill would seize the tools and execute at once any job that might be on hand.   That he would be engaged was a matter of course.   Who would lose the chance of securing such services as his ?   In this way he would travel from town to town, until he had completed the circuit of England.   What a glory for the Fenners !   And what an honour for himself, since none of his race, there was reason to believe, had ever before travelled farther than the county town !

He stopped first at Ilmington, where he experienced no difficulty in carrying out his plan, because the principal smith and wheelwright, a man named Thompson, had known his father, and for old acquaintance sake was glad to give his son a turn. But Ilmington was not at all to the taste of Mr. John Albert Fenner.   For a few days the novelty amused him, but this attraction was soon exhausted, and then he began to complain of the gloom and dirtiness of the town.   Its narrow, grimy streets were in startling contrast to the wide and radiant horizons which had spread before his eyes in his native district.   Again, the work was so heavy at Mr. Thompson's that there was no time for gossipping with customers and wayfarers, as at the Crossways ; and further, those who called conversed about persons and things of which John Albert Fenner knew nothing, and his ignorance in this respect John Albert Fenner found very annoying

At the end of a month he packed up his belongings and started for Adisham.   There he was less fortunate than at Ilmington, failed in five applications before he found a master willing to employ him, and then only on his own terms.   Treatment such as this greatly disgusted him with Adisham, and his disgust increased when he experienced the harshness of his new employer, who was not easily satisfied either as to the quality or quantity of his work.

As soon as he had saved a little money—not an easy matter, to be sure, when one's wages are small, and the cost of living high—John Albert Fenner bade a hasty farewell to Adisham. Sheffield was still the goal of his ambition, and thitherward he slowly bent his steps.   He stopped at Barton ; stopped there much longer than he had intended, for a difficulty arose in regard to his attire.   The rustic cut of his clothes had involved him in a good deal of ridicule at Adisham ; but it was much worse at Barton.   The street boys made a mark of him— "Who's your tailor ? "   " Oh, what a guy ! "   " Why don't you let yourself out for a scarecrow ! "   With these and similar contemptuous remarks they assailed the unfortunate John Albert Fenner, who observed, moreover, that people as they passed by looked at him with a smile, and turned round in order to give him another survey.   He tried to exchange his habiliments for a town-made suit, but though they were of better quality no second-hand clothes vendor would deal in them.   He was compelled, therefore, to endure the jibes and jests of the unfeeling until he had saved out of his wages a sufficient sum to pay for what he wanted.

At Thackham he spent three months, and then went on to Sheffield, where he expected to be welcomed with open arms, and to be paid at a rate which would fully compensate him for all he had lost and suffered. As soon as he had gathered up the necessary capital—in ten or twelve months, perhaps—he would start on his own account, and attracting all the custom of the place by his superior skill and agreeable manners, would soon be at the head of an army of workmen, attentive to his lightest commands. He was tired of being at the beck and call of surly fellows no better than, if as good as, himself, and wanted to play the much easier part (as he thought it) of master and employer. Then, when he was directing a large trade and living in a fine house, and was known and respected everywhere as Mr. John Albert Fenner, do you think he would be willing to return to the Crossways to shoe country horses and mend broken cart-wheels? Not a bit of it! He would pay them a visit now and then, dressed in his newest and best clothes, and his mother should be welcome to a five-pound note; but the Crossways business, such as it was, might be carried on, for all he cared, by one of his brothers. It was much too small an affair to be worth the attention of John Albert Fenner.

But in less than a month his vain-glorious dreams were rudely dispelled. He had heard that at Sheffield good workmen were always well paid. This was true enough when they found work to do, but John Albert Fenner failed to obtain any. There were scores of men, better workmen than himself, wandering from place to place in search of employment, and unable to secure it. What was he to do? Food was awfully dear, but to starve was unpleasant, and in spite of the most vigorous economy his small savings rapidly melted away. His clothes began to wear out—especially his boots, which his daily tramps from shop to shop, and forge to forge, put to a severer test than they were fitted to endure. Then his lodgings! Every week he was forced to find a cheaper bedroom, and at length he was glad to get a "shakedown" at threepence a night in a common lodging-house, with the prospect, in another week or two, of ·passing the night in the streets, the police-cell, or the work-house.

In fact, he was reduced almost to the last extremity, when Providence threw in his way a person whom he had known at Crayford, and, on some occasions, kindly treated. He was barman at a small public-house in one of the suburbs, and counted among his acquaintances a blacksmith, who fortunately happened just then to be in want of "a hand." He engaged John Albert Fenner; and though his wages were low, John Albert gladly accepted them, for they would suffice at all events to keep him from starvation. Here he had to shoe the broken-down horses of carters and small tradesmen, and to mend the wheels of the most wretched vehicles, so that he was forced to own to himself that he might much better have remained at Crossways Cottage. He toiled incessantly from morning until night, all the year round, for Bank-Holidays had not yet been invented; and, instead of looking out upon green meadows and clusters of leafy trees and cloudless skies, his weary eyes rested on a forest of tall and hideous factory chimneys and an impenetrable canopy of black smoke.

Oh! what a fool he had been! Why did he not remain at the Crossways? His illusions vanished one by one; his pride and conceit underwent a complete prostration; and he became a much wiser, if a sadder, man. "Home" was often in his thoughts, but how would he be received if he returned there? They would laugh at his folly, would rejoice in his humiliation, would exult over his defeat. They would say, "I told you so!" —the most aggravating words that can fall upon human ears. Besides, he would in all probability be "one too many;" he was not wanted. The business was not too much for his father to manage; and if it were, his brother Richard was old enough to help, and would in due time succeed to it. How strange it would seem! Richard Fenner, smith and wheelwright, breaking up the succession of "John Fenners" which had prevailed for centuries!

The thought elicited a deep sigh, and he felt as if he would give ten years of life to see once more the old house at home, and the time-honoured horse-shoe above the smithy door, and the wooden trough, under the great elm in front, where thirsty cattle quenched their summer thirst, and the big bellows which blew such a mighty draught of air, and the anvil which had rung with many a heavy blow from the hammers wielded by stalwart Fenners. Yes, ten years of life would be a small price to pay for so great a pleasure! He felt, under the influence of these emotions, as if he must start at once for Crayford and the Crossways, but a feeling of shame restrained him, and he toiled away at his unwelcome work in the grimy Sheffield suburb, with regret for the past, and weariness for the future.

One day, however, while drinking a glass of beer—how unlike the wholesome, amber-coloured ale brewed at the Crossways!— in the little public-house where his Crayford friend acted as barman, he met there a young soldier who had only recently joined

the ranks. He was a native of Spilsbury, and had often loitered
about the Crossways smithy while waiting for a horse to be shod
or a saw re-set. A few weeks before he had passed the cottage
on his way to Crayford, and he was able to give John Albert
some news which started him on his way home that very evening. He returned home as poor as when he left : he had not
discovered or mastered any of those wonderful secrets of the
smith's art with which his imagination had beguiled him ; but,
at no small cost, he had learned the folly of ambition—was
cured of restlessness and discontent—and was well inclined to
be content for the future with the hereditary fame and fortune
of the Fenners. His departure had greatly injured that fame
and fortune ; might his return prove the harbinger of more
prosperous days !

Yes, his departure had proved distinctly calamitous. For if
he had never left the Crossways, his strong right arm would
have held as in a vice the wayward, spirited horse which, breaking loose from the feeble hold of his brother Frank, had knocked
down the elder Fenner and broken his thigh. If John Albert
had been at home to take his father's place and conduct the
business, it would have gone on as prosperously as usual ;
whereas, now, the family were reduced to poverty, and it was
much feared that the cottage and the smithy would have to be
put up to auction and sold to the highest bidder.   John Albert
was profoundly moved when he thought of the cloud that had
come over his father's declining years, and reproached himself
bitterly for having indulged a "vaulting ambition" and a
mistaken pride.

It was with indescribable feelings of joy and gratitude that he
gazed once more on the gabled roof, and latticed casements,

and rose-embowered porch of his birth-place. As he approached
it he could hear the bells of Crayford ringing out a merry peal,
for it was the bell-ringers' practice-night, and their joyous sounds
seemed to fill his heart with new hope and courage. He
knocked the door; it was thrown open, and in a moment he
was in his mother's arms, while his right hand was heartily
grasped by his crippled father, and his left by his brother
Frank. John Albert had returned, and there was happiness
that night beneath John Fenner's roof. The only hen left in
the poultry-yard was sacrificed to do honour to the occasion,
for the wanderer was home again, and the world has always
shown itself strangely tender towards its prodigal sons! It is
for them, and not for the honest fellows who stay at home and
do their daily work always in the same steadfast but common-
place way that the fatted calf is killed!

The visitor to Crayford, if he ramble along the Winsham
Road for a mile or so, will find the cottage and its smithy still
standing in the old spot, with the tall elm in front, and over
the smithy door an alarming innovation, in the shape of a large
board, inscribed (in gold letters), "John Albert Fenner, Smith
and Wheelwright." John Albert worthily sustains the reputation of his ancestors, and is esteemed the best smith in all the
county. He has married happily, and is the father of a sturdy
boy and girl, who, with their good looks and restless ways, are
at once the pleasure and anxiety of their venerable grandfather
and grandmother. Whether he thinks the name of Albert an
ill-omened one for a member of the Fenner family I cannot
determine, but I know that his son bears no other name than
that of John Fenner the younger.

VII.

WOODSIDE: A STORY OF TRUE CHARITY.

WOODSIDE is acknowledged to be one of the prettiest estates in the neighbourhood of Crayford. It extends from the river Cray for a mile and a half or two miles towards Spilsbury, and includes within its ample boundaries almost every variety of English landscape—coppice and meadow, valley and green hills, cornfield and bosky dell, together with all the usual component parts of an English gentleman's demesne—a capital model farm, a game preserve, a fishing pond, a dairy farm, a couple of "lodges," a saw-mill, and picturesque groups of labourers' cottages. The house is a handsome and spacious building, with a centre and two wings, a colonnade, and a dignified-looking portico, separated from the park by a terrace and a ha-ha, and looking out from the state-rooms at the back on a fair expanse of garden, originally designed by the famous landscape-gardener, Capability Brown. For generations the estate had belonged to the Delameres; but the family had grown poorer and poorer, its sons being fond of high play and its daughters of high dress, until at last, to avert a scandal, it was sold for a very considerable sum to Mr. Westerton, the financier.

Mr. Westerton, having spent half his life in the acquisition of

money, had not had time as yet to grow weary of it. On retiring from business he wisely looked around for some pursuit
which might pleasantly occupy his leisure—a pursuit involving
no very great excitement, and he happily hit upon the collection
of coins and medals. It was a refined pursuit, and it was an
expensive one, conditions which perfectly suited Mr. Westerton,
so that when his friends complimented him on his skill as a
numismatist he was completely happy. He lavished a good
deal of money on his conservatories, his vineries, and his flower-
gardens, and at the Crayford horticultural show his fruits and
flowers always carried off the best prizes (for the benefit of his
gardeners). But the finest orchid or the most luscious peach
did not convey to him a tithe of the pleasure he experienced
from handling a rose-noble of the reign of Edward I., or a
denarius of the Emperor Tiberius.

As for Mrs. Westerton, she had no numismatic hobby. She
was a handsome, an exceedingly handsome woman, and like
most handsome women, she was fond of costly attire. A handsome woman, well-dressed, naturally wishes to be seen and
admired, and therefore Mrs. Westerton was fond of balls,
garden-parties, theatres, concerts, bazaars, and of all entertainments at which she could display her fine eyes and her diamonds,
her tall figure and her last Parisian costume. Perhaps she
might have been moved to better things if she had had children,
but no childish voices enlivened the echoes of the splendid
mansion at Woodside, and caring nothing for the resources of
art and culture, she was almost compelled to seek a succession
of gaieties to prevent her from succumbing to the weariness of
an unoccupied life.

It must be admitted, however, that she and her husband

were on the most cordial terms; but then, they did not see very much of each other, except in Society. They spent the season in London, and when they were at Woodside the house was filled with visitors. Still, they were regarded in Crayford, and all around Crayford, as models of conjugal affection. And the editor of *The Crayford Chronicle*, who was a poet as well as a journalist, and in both capacities was sometimes invited to a garden-party, or a state dinner, at Woodside, once printed, in large type, at the head of a conspicuous column of *The Chronicle*, some elegant verses, in which he alluded gracefully to this remarkable example of the bliss of matrimony, and declared that—

> " For generous spouse and lovely wife,
> The fates have wove the web of life
> With radiant threads of gold "—

a new and original idea, which stamped its creator as a great poetical genius. Mrs. Westerton expressed her gracious approval of Mr. De Laney's "sweet little poem," and ordered for her own behoof two hundred copies of the number of the paper in which it appeared. It is not every poet whose compositions meet with such immediate success.

The good people of Crayford were not blessed with faculties of keen perception and cool judgment, and knowing that the Westertons, besides their beautiful mansion at Woodside, had a fine house in Grosvenor Place, carriages, coachmen, footmen, gardeners, and all the accessories of wealth, were never weary of commenting upon their " unclouded happiness." "Unclouded happiness "—that was the beautiful phrase—coined, of course, by the editor of *The Crayford Chronicle*. For a wonder, this external criticism, pronounced by persons who were not critics,

I

was actually correct. The owners of Woodside were almost incredibly happy—as happy as that king of whom one reads in ancient story, whose prosperousness so alarmed a thoughtful friend, that he advised the happy monarch to sacrifice something valuable by way of propitiating Fortune. They were happy with " unclouded happiness " until the day when—but we must not anticipate.

*   *   *   *   *

A garden-party at Marlborough House. A pretty young creature, graceful as a fawn, radiant as day, after a prolonged stare at Mrs. Westerton, who moved among the crowd, tall and majestic, like a Juno, remarked to the gentleman in attendance upon her—" That woman must once have been wonderfully handsome ! " (" Once ! " what an impertinence—the impertinence of Truth !) With a courtly bow, and a dainty trick of phrase, not very common on the lips of the young men of to-day, the gentleman replied, " Autumn, however gorgeous it may be, can never hope to rival the charms of Spring." Ah, what an elegant compliment ! So fresh ! so novel ! so poetical ! Happy is the man who can make compliments. But is it not a lost art ?

To the surprise of her princely host, the lady of Woodside retired very much earlier than was her custom, and, as she drove home, revealed a certain amount of irritability, which she endeavoured to excuse on the plea that she had a severe headache. Her husband, who had met at Marlborough House with another numismatic enthusiast, and had received the promise of a half-farthing of Ethelred the Redeless, was in such a state of beaming good humour, that his wife's pettishness passed by unnoticed. But, on reaching home, she got rid of her *mauvaise humeur* on her two maids, Jane and Alice, who retired from her presence discomposed. " She seems to have a bad nervous attack," said Jane. " What *can* have put missus in such a temper ? " inquired Alice. The outbreak provoked a severe comment in the servants' hall, where the faults and follies of the drawing-room are always mercilessly criticized.

Not long after this affair, our Crayford poet broke out into verse in praise of Autumn, in which his patroness fancied she detected the sting of an epigram concealed in the honey of his rhymes. The next time she met him, she treated the unfortunate man with such haughty indifference, and threw at him such disdainful glances, that he went back to his office more than half inclined to compose a satire on the Mutability of Women, and dedicate it to Mrs. Westerton, of Woodside.

Suddenly our heroine—for such she is, and a great deal better than any of Ouida's or Miss Broughton's—began to detest the town and adore the country. "God made the country," she said, quoting Cowper, "and man made the town." But she was no sooner at Woodside than she wanted to be back in London. She would not confess it, but solitude weighed heavily upon her. She had no resources in herself; and except *Myra's Journal*, or *The Queen*, or the last fashionable novel, she read nothing. Much reading was bad for the eyes, and affected her nerves. Yet she shrank from re-appearing in Society, lest somebody else, besides the rude young cavalier at the Prince's Garden party, should compare her—to Autumn ! Autumn—the season of decay ! And she was only—forty. Fortunate was it for Mr. Westerton that he was absorbed in the compilation of a paper on the William the Conqueror fourpenny-piece for the Numismatical Society, or he would have

been driven crazy—perhaps rendered ill-tempered—by her
caprices. It is sometimes a good thing when one's husband
rides a hobby.

* * * * *

The season was over, and "the Drive" in Hyde Park
deserted. Everybody who was anybody had left London, and
the Westertons, being somebodies, left it also. At Woodside
the scene was charming. Along the terraces bloomed rows of
the choicest flowers ; purple grapes hung in rich clusters in the
vinery ; exotics of rare beauty bloomed in the conservatories ;
the woods were in glorious leaf, though just tinged with the
fine Autumnal colours ; and from afar came the voices of the
reapers as they toiled among the corn. Human nature could
not be utterly indifferent to this magnificent display. James,
the butler, stood on the steps of the portico, and surveyed with
well-pleased eye his master's demesne. Alice, from one of the
upper windows, held merry converse with a good-looking young
gardener who was mowing the tennis ground ; and Jane chirped
in the gladness of her heart as she arranged the contents of her
lady's extensive wardrobe. The glad contagion infected even
the owner of Woodside, who, attracted by the sunshine, quitted
his study and his cabinets, and sauntered along the corridor to
the tune of an air from " Ruddigore," caught up, during his
sojourn in London, from a wandering barrel-organ.

He crossed the drawing-room, and stepped out into the
conservatory. Why did he cease his whistling and draw back
a step or two ? Because, to his surprise, his wife stood there,
with gloom on her brow, and in her hand a blossom, from which
she was slowly picking the delicate petals one by one. She had

sought the glittering "hall of glass" that she might meditate at her leisure on the unwelcome aphorism dropped from careless lips at that memorable garden party :—"Autumn, however gorgeous, cannot rival the charms of Spring."

Observing her husband's retrograde movement, she drily said—

"Do I frighten you, Stephen?"

Mr. Westerton was blessed with a sudden inspiration—

"Impossible, my dear!   It is your privilege to attract."

Mrs. Westerton smiled incredulously, and retorted—

"No, speak the truth, Stephen.   Seeing me here in the blaze of sunlight, you were startled at the wrinkles, the sunken cheeks, the dim eyes, the various signs that I am growing "— she could not bring herself to utter the awful words, "an old woman," so she substituted the scarcely less painful one— "ugly!"   And she flung her flower away with a gesture of impatience.

"Ugly! Ugly! You, my dear! What are you thinking of? You are as handsome as ever—no, even handsomer than on the day you made me the happiest of men!   Go, and look at yourself in your glass, my love!"

I think that, for a numismatist, this was a very pretty speech, and Mr. Westerton meant it.   To his fond eyes his wife shone with the charm of unchanging beauty.

But Mrs. Westerton *had* consulted her glass—only too often. She had consulted it so long and so frequently, and in so unhappy a mood, that one or two lines on her fair forehead she had magnified into wrinkles, and a few grey hairs among her raven-black masses she had accepted as symptoms of coming baldness.   It is true that the fine curves of her cheeks had relaxed a little, and that her eyes were not so sparkling, perhaps, as they had been twenty years before. It was true that she was entering on the autumnal period of her beauty ; but, so far, there was very little change, and as years had matured her form and developed the expression of her fine features, her husband was not wrong when he had declared that she was handsomer even than in her youth.

Her sole answer, however, to his affectionate words was to sweep past him with the air of an outraged queen, never condescending to bestow on the unfortunate man a smile or a glance, and, with a firm and measured step, to seek the solitude of her boudoir.

＊　　＊　　＊　　＊　　＊

Thenceforward Mrs. Westerton's temper became so irritable that everybody at Woodside suffered dreadfully. Jane was in tears from morning to night, and Alice wore on her countenance an air of settled gloom which struck terror to the young gardener's susceptible heart. The butler grew so confused that he decanted the wrong wines on the very day that his master entertained the Bishop of Z. to dinner. The editor of *The Crayford Chronicle* was so severely snubbed when he presented himself with some new poems, and asked permission to dedicate them to the lady of Woodside, that he did not recover his spirits for a month, and during that period alarmed his readers by despairing " editorials," which foretold the break-up of the British Empire and the ruin of Crayford. As for Mr. Westerton, he was so wounded by her continual raillery at his love of " rubbishy old coins "—good gracious ! a denarius of Heliogabalus and a farthing of Edward the Confessor to be thus shamefully aspersed !—that he begun to loathe his collection, and gave Messrs. Puttick and Simpson instructions to dispose of it by auction. The sale was a nine day's wonder, and the pecuniary result proved to demonstration that "rubbishy" old coins may be worth a good many new ones.

Mr. Westerton, however, could not be happy without a hobby, and having given up his occupation as a numismatist, he next turned entomologist, and addressed himself to the task of filling glass cases with impaled butterflies, beetles, moths, and the like—a cheaper amusement than collecting old coins.

His wife, meanwhile, tried ever so many different ways of getting rid of the time that weighed on her hands so heavily, now that she no longer spent hours before her mirror, or changed her toilette half-a-dozen times a day. She tried riding, but soon grew tired of trotting up and down the same roads and lanes. She went shopping, but Crayford contained little that pleased her fastidious taste. An aviary occupied her for a week or two, and then she took a sudden fancy for painting. After she had daubed an acre of canvas with highly-coloured views of Wood-side from the lake, Woodside from the Gothic ruins, Woodside from the terrace, Woodside from the gardens, and so on, she threw aside her palette and her brushes, and thought she would improve her mind by reading. The volume she caught up purported to have been written by a Woman for Women, and she turned over its pages eagerly, in the hope she might find some recipe for resisting the advance of Old Age. "Autumn is bad enough," she exclaimed, "but when Winter comes, what then?" Mrs. Westerton shuddered.

The first passage that caught her eye ran thus—

"Women who have lived wholly in the amusements and

pursuits of Society become sensible of a great void as they advance in years. The world ignores them, and common sense tells them that they ought to ignoré the world."

(" That does not apply to me," thought Mrs. Westerton, " for I am as much sought after as ever. Three invitations to balls and two to lawn-tennis parties came this morning.")

She went on reading—

" What, then, are they to do ? The Past awakens regret."

(Mrs. Westerton sighed.)

" The Present teems with vexations."

(" True, very, very true ! No one knows what I suffer and no one pities me ! ")

" The Future is heavy with fears ! "

(" Oh, bother the Future ! I shall be dead of *ennui* long before it arrives.")

Turning over a page or two, she read—

" Brief is the reign of beauty, and nothing more melancholy than the later life of women who have been beauties, and nothing else."

(" Well, but what is the remedy ? " exclaimed Mrs. Westerton. "What are we poor beauties to do, when Autumn cannot rival the charms of Spring ? I thank thee, sir, for teaching me those words ! What are we to do, I say ? ")

" When you live only for the pleasures of the world, and these fail you, either because your taste for them passes away, or because your reason detects their worthlessness, you feel a great want."

(" That is most true. But how are we to supply it ? ")

And Mrs. Westerton, throwing aside the book, began to think.

" Yes, how am I to supply the want of which I am fully conscious? By religion? Well, I go to Church once every Sunday, and sometimes twice ; I give to all the parish charities, and I never *will* consent to go on a Sunday to a lawn-tennis party. No ; Sunday is a day of rest, and I don't even take out my horses on Sunday.

" By charity? Everybody knows that there is not a poor person on my husband's estate. I could not bear to see people going about in rags ! And Jane could tell you that when any-body is ill she is always sent off at once with a bottle of wine, or a jelly, or something nice and nourishing ; and last Christ-mas I gave away four-and-twenty pairs of boots and as many blankets.

" By work? Oh, bother ! I don't care for embroidery, or stitching, or sewing, or whatever you call it ! It weakens the eyesight, which I am sure is a very wrong thing to do—and besides, I pay Jane and Alice to do it for me.

" Reading? Well, I will try it. I always *do* read a good novel, when I have time for it. I read all the Jubilee odes, and poor stuff I thought them ; but now I will try steady, solid reading. What shall I begin with ? I suppose one ought to know something about history, so I will go down to the library and ask Stephen for—but, oh dear me ! it is nearly dinner-time, and I have not been out to-day. Where is Alice ? I think I will put off the history until to-morrow."

*　　　*　　　*　　　*　　　*

A few minutes later Mrs. Westerton, charmingly attired, and attended by Alice, appeared on the terrace. She crossed the ha-ha by a little rustic bridge, and strolled along until she came to a plantation, which Mr. Westerton had designed as a protection for the house against easterly winds. She was about to turn off in the direction of the home-farm, when one of the labourers on the estate rushed out of the plantation with a pale face and every sign of alarm.

"What is the matter, Simpson?" inquired Mrs. Westerton, hastily.

Simpson stopped for a moment, touched his hat, wiped his face, and said, "An accident, ma'am! Very bad, indeed, ma'am! Poor Joe!"

And again touching his hat, off he went.

"Alice, go and see what the silly fellow means," said her mistress; and Alice, very reluctantly, made a step or two into the plantation. In a moment she was back at her mistress's side.

"Oh, ma'am! he's dead! I am sure he is."

"Who's dead?" inquired Mrs. Westerton, startled.

"Poor Joe, ma'am! The widow's son—she lives in the little cottage by the saw-mill, you know, ma'am. You always liked the boy, ma'am."

Without waiting for another word, Mrs. Westerton—who was by no means deficient either in courage or intelligence when she chose to put off her affectations, and forget that she had a reputation of a beauty to maintain—entered the coppice; and there, among the bracken and dead leaves, at the foot of a young beech, lay a boy of fourteen or fifteen years of age. While lopping off a dead branch, he had lost his balance, and fallen; and fallen with such a crash that he was completely doubled up, his head bent in upon his chest. His face was covered with a deathly pallor; his eyes were closed; and a thin stream of blood trickled from his lips.

Fine lady as she was, Mrs. Westerton did not faint. She called to Alice to run to the house for brandy, and with her vinaigrette endeavoured to recall the poor boy to consciousness. Simpson returning to the spot with three of his fellow-workmen, she despatched one of them to Crayford for the doctor, ordering him to mount the swiftest horse in the stables, and sent another to apprise her husband of the sad occurrence. Simpson had brought a can of water, in which she dipped her handkerchief, and applied it to the boy's forehead; at the same time moistening his lips, and wiping away the blood—all this with a wonderful tenderness and a light, soft, caressing touch. On the arrival of Alice with the brandy, she poured a little down the lad's throat, Simpson holding up his head for the purpose. In a few minutes, she mixed a little with water, and gave it to him; after which, with many a gasp and laboured breath he struggled back into consciousness, fixing his eyes upon his mistress with a pathetic look of gratitude.

"Thank you, ma'am," he said, in low broken tones; "'tis real good of you; but I be badly hurt."

"My poor boy," said his mistress, "are you in much pain?"

"Not much pain, ma'am," he said slowly and with evident effort, "but I feel bad."

"We must carry him to the house at once, Simpson," observed Mrs. Westerton; but when the men attempted to raise him, he shrieked with agony, and exclaimed that his back was broken. As he was on the point of fainting again, they desisted. Mrs. Westerton ordered the construction of a litter, and, under her direction, half a dozen young ash poles were rapidly tied together; some straight fir branches woven in among them ; and upon this framework was accumulated a thick layer of moss and dead leaves. After administering another small dose of brandy to poor Joe, she instructed the men to make with their handkerchiefs a couple of slings, one of which was placed under his limbs, and the other under his shoulders ; she then supported his head in her arms, and in this way, slowly and gently, he was got upon the litter. Raising it from the ground they proceeded with slow and measured steps to the house, Mr. Westerton meeting them on the way. He was surprised, but not a little delighted, at the sympathy and sagacity his wife had displayed ; and after sending off a messenger to Joe's mother, listened in silent admiration to the wise and tender words with which, while holding his rough hand in her delicate white palms, she sought to cheer and console the sufferer. The truth is, Mrs. Westerton was endowed with a noble heart and fine nature, which had been oppressed and obscured by a frivolous education and a frivolous life. She was ignorant of her real self, of her true individuality ; but her eyes having been opened by this sad incident, her husband hoped that their clear vision would never again be obstructed.

When the doctor arrived, he pronounced the dreadful verdict that the case was hopeless. Besides undergoing internal injuries, poor Joe had broken his spine, and the lower extremities were already paralysed. We shall not dwell upon the grief of his poor mother, for its intensity was almost indescribable. Mrs. Westerton shared it, and wept bitterly while the two were taking their last farewell. From her Prayer Book she read such of the Collects and Psalms as seemed best fitted for the occasion; not without a painful feeling that her vain and empty life of pleasure had ill fitted her to minister by the bedside of the dying, and soothe and encourage him on his passage across the dark waters of Jordan. In that solemn hour the follies of the course she had pursued were brought home to her with startling force, and she vowed that, if the opportunity were given her in the future, she would make a wiser use of the means Heaven had placed at her disposal.

She remained by poor Joe to the last, and helped his mother to compose the contorted limbs and close the glazing eyes. Then she retired to her room, and sat alone for upwards of an hour, conscious that a great change had come upon her, revolutionizing all her thoughts, feelings, and hopes.

A new and excellent method of employing her leisure had been opened up to her—that of practical and personal charity. Not the ostentatious benevolence which publishes its donations in the newspapers, or doles out its alms by official hands; but the living, vigorous, wide-hearted generosity which seeks the sick and destitute in their homes, and carries thither not only the helping hand, but the sympathising and consoling voice. Thenceforward Mrs. Westerton never felt the minutes hang idly on her hands; for of all the philanthropic work in and around Crayford, she was the heart and head, as intelligent as she was liberal. The education of the young, the reform of the criminal, the relief of the indigent—these were the objects of her activity, and they left her no leisure hours to give up to the frivolities of Society. She grew handsomer every day, her countenance assuming a new expression of refinement and grace, but she quite forgot that she had ever been a beauty. And the blessings of grateful hearts proved more delightful to her ears than ever had done the flatteries of all her admirers.

VIII.

PROSPECT HOUSE : A STORY OF OLD WAYS AND NEW WAYS.

I.

IF you have ever visited Crayford, you will probably remember the large white house that stands on the high ground above the bridge, with its pillared façade looking towards the river. It is called Prospect House, and appropriately enough, for it commands "a prospect," not less extensive than varied, of the valley of the Cray for several miles, and of the low green hills, so richly wooded, which raise their undulating crests against the western horizon. A commodious and handsome mansion, surrounded by pleasant grounds, it is the residence of Mr. Morton, an old-established solicitor, and the confidential adviser of nearly all the "county" families.

There, in a large airy apartment fitted up as a schoolroom—which opened into a conservatory, and *that* into a spacious garden—sat, one summer afternoon, Mr. Morton's two daughters, Matilda, aged thirteen, and Florence, aged eleven, along with their governess, Miss Simperson. Matilda and Florence were pretty English blondes, moderately clever, and with good dispositions—that is, they were seldom intentionally troublesome,

they were easily led, and they generally spoke the truth. Their
governess was quite a young woman in years ; but, somehow or
other, teachers soon get to wear a look of age, and Miss
Simperson's forehead, receding beneath a mass of dull red hair,
was a complete net-work of wrinkles. Charles Morton, a saucy
Rugby lad, declared that it reminded him of a railway map of
Great Britain. As she lowered her glasses—these young gover-
nesses almost always wear glasses, as the insignia, I suppose of
their profession—over the exercise books ot her two pupils, any
person seeing her for the first time would have put her down to
be a woman of thirty-five, and yet she was ten years younger !
She was, however, a warm-hearted little woman and an accomplished teacher.

"Your dictation is fairly well done, Matilda," she said,
addressing the elder sister; " very neatly written, and with
only two mistakes."

"Two mistakes, ma'am ! Oh, I made sure there were none ! "

" Yes, two, look for yourself. You have spelt "rhinoceros "
without the _h_, and omitted one of the p's from "hippopotamus !"

"Oh, ma'am, I don't call _them_ mistakes ! They are just hard
words from that odious Natural History."

" As they must be corrected, they are of course errors."

"Then I shall lose the new half-crown Papa promised me if
I made no mistake in my spelling."

"Perhaps you will do better to-morrow," remarked Miss
Simperson. "But why do you wish so much to get the half-
crown ? "

"Well, I want to buy a lot of things ! "

"A lot of things," said Miss Simperson, smiling, " with half-
a-crown ?"

"Yes, little socks and shoes for widow Brown's poor little grandchild, ma'am."

"Go on with your lessons then, and I daresay you will soon win a reward from Mr. Morton."

Her two pupils drew their books towards them, and had just begun to resume their work with energy, when the door opened, and in rushed Bertha Brandon. On perceiving Miss Simperson, she stopped short, and timidly exclaimed —

"Oh, ma'am, will you, will you let me hide myself here? Mrs. Creevet is looking for me everywhere."

"But, my child," said the governess mildly, "it is wrong of you to hide, if Mrs. Creevet wants you. You ought to go and meet her."

"Oh no, ma'am, she wants to shut me up in the black hole. Alice is in there already: she let Mrs. Creevet catch her, but I contrived to get away."

Here Matilda spoke.

"Why does Mrs. Creevet want to shut up you and Alice in that horrid closet?"

"Because she is always spiting us. She pretends that we don't hold ourselves upright, and wants to make us work with a steel girdle and backboards, which give us frightful pains, and prevent us from moving our head or our arms. She says that these horrid things were worn by all young ladies when she was a child. If so, I am awfully glad I wasn't a young lady then! So my dear, dear, dear cousins—and you, too, good Miss Simperson—do hide me, I beg of you."

Miss Simperson was much distressed, for she did not approve of the harsh measures adopted by Mrs. Creevet, but, at the same time, she could not openly encourage or countenance the child in disobeying her aunt. So she compromised the matter with her conscience by retiring to her own room, and leaving her pupils to assist their cousin if they chose.

And they *did* choose! They persuaded her to get under the table at which they were writing. It was covered with a cloth so large that it touched the floor. Then one snatched up a book and the other a pencil, and had just re-seated themselves when in swept the dreaded aunt. Looking all about the room with suspicious eyes, she exclaimed—

"So you are alone, young ladies. Is no one with you ? "

"Miss Simperson, ma'am," replied Matilda, " has just gone to her room."

" Alone ? "

"Yes, ma'am, alone," said Florence, slily kicking Bertha under the table cover.

"Well, you don't do much work in her absence," growled Mrs. Creevet, leaning over them.

"What makes you think so, ma'am ?" quietly asked Matilda.

" Because you are holding your book upside down, Matilda, which is *not* favourable to diligent study."

Matilda, blushing, re-adjusted her French Grammar.

"And you, Florence, have chosen a lead pencil with which to continue an exercise begun with pen and ink."

Florence threw down her pencil, and replaced it by a pen.

" And how embarrassed you look ! Evidently you have been doing something wrong. Ah, this comes of spoiling children ! When you are allowed to have all your own way, the consequences are most deplorable."

Here Matilda thought it necessary to speak up for herself and her sister.

K

"Both mamma and Miss Simperson are pleased with us, ma'am, and I don't think you have any right to find fault with the education they provide."

"An education"—this was said with an elevation of Mrs. Creevet's fine Roman nose—"which makes you so very polite and attractive! Hum, ha! If _I_ had the bringing of you up, I would take care that you learned the rules of good behaviour."

"Yes, and then we should be as wretched as now we are happy," said Matilda.

"And as naughty and idle as Bertha and Alice are growing," chimed in Florence.

"That's untrue," suddenly interrupted Bertha, from under the table. "I'm as good as gold when Aunt Creevet's away."

"What is that? Hum, ha! _Now_ I know the cause of your confusion and impertinence. Come out from your hiding-place, you bad girl, and follow me."

But while Mrs. Creevet was speaking, Bertha slipped out of her asylum, and, on her hands and knees, softly crawled across the floor until she reached the door opening into the conservatory, where she suddenly disappeared. Her aunt waited a minute or two, and, the culprit not appearing, lifted up the cloth, but, to her intense mortification, the bird had flown.

"What is this? Why, she was here but a moment ago; I am confident I heard her under the table. Matilda, Florence—I insist that you tell me where your cousin is."

"I cannot tell you, ma'am," said Matilda, smiling, "because I don't know."

"But you _do_ know, you _must_ know. Where has she gone, miss?"

" I assure you, madam," said Florence, laughing, " that we don't know any more than you. Had you not better try to find her ? "

" Very well, young ladies, very well. Yes, I *shall* try to find her, and when I have found her I shall punish her as she deserves."

And in a storm of indignation she swept out of the room. As soon as she was out of hearing, the two girls, I am sorry to say, burst out laughing.

" Well, this is very funny," said Matilda. " How did Bertha escape ? "

" I don't know," answered Florence. " I was looking at Mrs. Creevet, and wondering at the extraordinary grimaces she made, so that I did not see Bertha go out."

" I expect she escaped through the garden door."

" I do not think so," said Florence; " Mrs. Creevet would have seen her."

" No, there she is—yonder, in the shrubbery."

" So she is ! Well, she is safe for the moment. Poor Alice ! I am sorry for her, shut up in that dark closet, with a board tied to her back, which hurts her every time she bends her head. I shall make an attempt to release her. Will you wait here for me ? I shall be back in a minute."

It is necessary here to explain that Mrs. Morton and Mrs. Brandon, who were sisters, had gone to Scarborough on a short visit for the benefit of Mrs. Morton's health. As Mr. Brandon at the time was on the Continent, engaged in some important commercial negotiations, the little Brandons had been invited to spend a few weeks with their cousins at Prospect House, and in the absence of their mother and aunt, Mrs. Creevet, their aunt on the paternal side, had taken charge of them. Unfortunately, her ideas of education and of the management of children were wholly derived from the experience of her childhood, when fear, not love, was the controlling influence, and much more time was devoted to the acquisition of what was called "deportment" than to the cultivation of the mind and the development of the affections; and she had already contrived to earn the dislike and forfeit the confidence of her nieces and their cousins.

When Florence returned with the poor little victim of her aunt's mistaken notions, she and Matilda lost no time in unfastening the board, and belt, and braces, and other appliances of torture with which she had been invested. Then arose the all-important question, what should they do with her? The discussion thereupon was abruptly terminated by the re-appearance of Mrs. Creevet, and Alice was hastily thrust into the garden, with strict injunctions from her cousins to find out Bertha and remain with her until they could get rid of "the Gorgon" (the shocking expression which, I am sorry to say, they applied to Mrs. Creevet).

As for "the Gorgon," she stalked into the schoolroom with her Roman nose higher in the air than ever, and her majestic brow heavy with gloom! Throwing herself into Miss Simperson's arm-chair, and fanning herself with her handkerchief, she exclaimed—

"This is truly incredible! To dare to make me run, and in this weather, too! Phew! I never, never saw such disgraceful behaviour in all my life. In *my* young days nothing of the kind would have been possible; but young ladies *were* young ladies then. (Turning towards Matilda and Florence

with a severe look.) And you, young ladies, who have encouraged the insolence of your cousin Bertha, you shall be
punished also. I shall demand it of Miss Simperson !"

"As we are not to blame, ma'am," replied Matilda, calmly,
"I feel sure Miss Simperson will not comply with your
request."

"Not to blame, Miss Impertinence ? Not to blame ! when
you assist your cousin to elude and evade my justice ! "

"Justice !" exclaimed Matilda, and then stopped suddenly.

"Well, miss, what do you wish to say ? "

"I would remind you of all the horrible things you made my
poor cousins wear. How do you think they can do their lessons
cramped by boards and braces, and all the rest of it ? "

"Ho, ho ! since you are so well informed, Miss Arrogance,
it is clear you have seen Bertha—that you have talked with her,
that you know where she is, that you helped her to hide, and
that you are as guilty, as criminal, as she is ! "

At this moment Miss Simperson entered, her cool and composed manner contrasting pleasantly with Mrs. Creevet's feverish
indignation. Mrs. Creevet immediately addressed her, with a
stern request that she would punish her two pupils, and
especially "that most insolent Matilda," in an exemplary
fashion. The governess naturally asked of what the young
ladies had been guilty, and when she had listened to their
aunt's impassioned harangue, suggested that she should let the
matter drop, as it was evident, on her own showing, that they
had not been concerned in Miss Brandon's escape. As for
herself, she had no idea where that young lady had concealed
herself, nor was it any business of hers. More angry words
from Mrs. Creevet as she quitted the schoolroom to pursue her

quest of the missing Bertha, and the governess was left alone with her pupils.

"I am sorry," said Miss Simperson, "that your cousins should have been left in charge of a lady so unfitted to guide and control them; but not the less do I feel that they are bound to obey her, both as their relative and as the guardian appointed by their mother. Where are they now?"

"I really do not know, ma'am, I assure you," said Matilda. "After you left us Bertha hid herself under the table, but was imprudent enough to speak, and Mrs. Creevet then ordered her to leave her hiding-place. As she made no sign, Mrs. Creevet looked under the table, but she was gone. And then her aunt accused me and Florence of having hidden her, though we did not know where or how she had made her escape. I suppose, however, that she crept on her hands and knees to the French window and slipped out into the garden. As for Alice, Florence went upstairs and released her, and then we sent her into the garden to find Bertha."

"I feel uneasy about them," said Miss Simperson, "and I think you had better go and look for both your cousins and bring them back."

Matilda and Florence had scarcely left the schoolroom for this purpose when Mrs. Creevet re-appeared, to the great annoyance of the unfortunate governess. She had been unable to find her missing niece, and had discovered that Alice was also absent. The servants had scoured the garden and grounds without coming upon any trace of the fugitives, and their aunt was thoroughly frightened—a prey to the gloomiest conjectures and the most startling apprehensions.

"I am sorry for you, ma'am," said Miss Simperson, "for this

kind of anxiety is terrible when one has so much responsibility upon one's shoulders, and more particularly when——"

" More particularly what?" snapped Mrs. Creevet, observing that the governess hesitated.

" More particularly when one might, perhaps, by more mild-ness and moderation, have escaped it. Excuse me, ma'am, if I say that, in my opinion at least, your system of management is dangerous, and, I will add, pernicious."

"I am surprised, Miss Simperson," exclaimed Mrs. Creevet, loftily, "that so young a person should presume to oppose her crude theories to the mature results of my long experience. Severity is necessary with children—take my word for it—or they will grow up disobedient, impertinent, idle, untruthful. The principles of education in vogue at the present day are simply shocking; but, of course, are just what might be expected in this Socialistic and Communistic age, when reverence is wholly unknown, and the distinctions of classes are being swept away by the flood-tide of Democracy. Hum, ha!"

And Mrs. Creevet fanned herself with a majestic air, as if her utterances had completely settled the question.

"But how is it, ma'am," said the governess, "that my dear pupils, whom I never punish and seldom scold, are so obedient, industrious, amiable, and good, while Bertha and Alice—who are being scolded and punished incessantly—are so trouble-some, and every day become more difficult to manage and more intractable?"

"Because, Miss Simperson, they are under my charge for six months only, and feel that they are sustained in their gross disobedience by their maid, their cousins, yes, and—I grieve to say it—by yourself, Miss Simperson."

"The insinuation respecting myself, ma'am, I pass unnoticed. But let me remind you that two years ago I saw a good deal of the Misses Brandon, for they spent six months here with their aunt, and they were then very good and exceedingly sweet-tempered. A change for the worse began when you first applied your old-world system of management, and——"

"I insist, Miss Simperson, that you cease these injurious reflections. My object, ma'am, is to teach them refinement of manners, grace and dignity of demeanour, a spirit of prompt and silent obedience, and in this I should succeed if they were placed in my care for a sufficiently long period. But, ma'am, these naughty children are apparently not to be found! What *can* have become of them? They may have fallen into the fish-pond, or into the river—agonizing thought!"

She rose, and moved towards the French window, when a voice apparently from beneath the table exclaimed—

"Don't alarm yourself, aunt! We are both all right."

You may imagine how great was the surprise both of Mrs. Creevet and the governess. Each hastened to the table, and lifted up the cover, but their surprise was increased when they found no one there. What Mrs. Creevet would have said or done I will not allow myself to conjecture, but the entrance of Matilda and Florence caused a diversion. The two girls said that they had found Alice in the garden, but she had not seen, nor could they see, the fugitive Bertha.

"A moment ago," said Miss Simperson, "she spoke to us from under the table, yet when we looked she was not there."

"Not there!" exclaimed Matilda; "then how did she pass you? I declare she reminds one of the Invisible Lady."

Miss Simperson observed that she would speak to Thompson,

the gardener, who would know, perhaps, what had become of her, and went out for the purpose, accompanied by Mrs. Creevet, who was genuinely uneasy. As they left the room by one door, Bertha thrust her head in at the other, inquiring, in a low voice, "Has she gone? Yes, I see the coast is clear, and, thank goodness, I am safe." And she danced into the room.

"Why, where *have* you been, you naughty girl?" exclaimed Alice. "What a fuss and bother your absence has been the cause of!"

"In the conservatory all the time, my dear! Here—close to the door."

"But how *could* you be there? Your aunt and I both looked into the conservatory, and saw nothing of you," rejoined Matilda.

"I *was* there, most worthy cousin, and I saw *you*—Had you been alone, I should have spoken—Do you see those bushy geraniums in the corner? I was behind them—Ha, ha, ha!"

"But the pots were in their proper order—not one was displaced."

"Of course not, because Thompson put them back after he had made room for me behind them."

"Oh, the gardener helped you?"

"Yes," said Bertha, "you know the jolly old fellow takes a pleasure in getting us out of our scrapes."

"But tell me," said Matilda, "why you hid yourself under the table a second time?"

"Oh, I was tired of crouching down in that damp corner; I was all pins and needles! So I got back into this room, intending to prevent you from looking for me any further; when, lo and behold, in flounced aunt, and didn't I just drop down under the table as if I had been shot!"

" What made you run the risk of being found out by speaking ?" inquired Matilda.

" Because," replied Bertha, "I had heard the conversation between my aunt and Miss Simperson, and discovered what a tremendous fright she was in—thinking I might have drowned myself, out of desperation, (as if I was so foolish, when mamma returns to-morrow !) So I ventured on a bit of a surprise for her—and oh, didn't she jump !—and then, before she recovered herself, I was down on my hands and knees, and back into the conservatory."

" Well, you must be hungry now," said Matilda ; " lunch time has passed long ago."

" No ; I had some grapes in the conservatory, and they were jolly nice, I assure you—But here comes Thompson ! Oh, and he has brought Alice with him.   Glad to see you, Thompson."

"So *you* are all right, miss ; that's good.   And here's Miss Alice, tired to death with running.   I wish your aunt, young ladies, if I may make bold to say so, wouldn't worrit you so— Forty-five years have I been in the service of your father and your father's father, and I have seen you all born, and all grow up like my tall fuchsias, and anything I can do for your father's children, it makes me happy to do."

" Then, first, you must get rid of this horrible machine which aunt fastens on our poor bodies 'to make us sit and walk upright,' she says !   Next, you must go up to the closet on the first landing, and there you will find another machine of the same kind, which you must also destroy."

" Hem, hem," coughed Thompson, "I shall gladly put that dreadful "ingin" out of the way ; but to go raking about a closet is quite another thing."

"Why, Thompson, why?" inquired Bertha.

"Because it has a sort of—sort of—clan—clan—"

"Clandestine," suggested Alice.

"—clandestine character; looks, in fact, very like—stealing."

"Oh no, no, not at all, Thompson," exclaimed Miss Brandon, "we order you to do it, don't you see? and if Aunt Creevet gets hold of that machine, she will put it on us, and you have no idea how it hurts—hurts back, and shoulders, and chest, and chin."

"But, Bertha," interrupted Matilda, "if this goes against Thompson's conscience, we had much better look for the thing ourselves."

"And if aunt catches us at it, what then?"

"Ah, indeed, indeed, who knows what such a harbitrary old lady might do? No, *I* must do it—I must fetch the ingin— and—I'll go at once."

In a few moments—at least, so it seemed to the expectant girls—Thompson returned, looking exceedingly pale and troubled. With a sensitiveness not always or often found in men of his class, he felt as if he had committed a crime, but he owned that, crime or not, he would do it again for the sake of his young ladies. He was on the point of departing with the two machines of torture, which, Matilda said, reminded her of the instruments used by the Inquisition, when the door opened, and in burst the ubiquitous Mrs. Creevet, followed by Miss Simperson. Bertha and Alice Brandon gave a scream, and made towards the garden, but Mrs. Creevet interposed her tall person, and in her most imperious tone, and with the loftiest possible elevation of her Roman nose, commanded them to remain where they were. Then she locked the door opening

•

from the hall, and put the key in her pocket, and, informing them that they would have to resume their "deportment apparatus," as she called it, she passed into the garden, locking after her the door of the conservatory.

"Well," said Thompson, concealing his spoils behind his back, "this is a complete take-in. We are caught like rats in a trap, and what on earth am I to do with these 'ingins'?"

"What 'ingins,' Thompson?" said Miss Simperson, laughing.

"Excuse me, ma'am; I forgot you was present. It was a little joke of mine with the young ladies."

"What is the bundle you are so carefully trying to hide behind your back, Thompson? How is this? Is everybody dumb? What is the matter?"

"If you please, ma'am," and Thompson, in much distress, scratched his head with his disengaged hand, and shifted his feet uneasily, "it is—you see—I am not young—I have my old ways—excuse my leaving you, ma'am, but of course I am out of my place in the young ladies' room."

"But what have you behind your back, Thompson?" inquired Miss Simperson, smiling.

"Oh, something, ma'am, not of much consequence—you will believe me, I know."

"But what *is* the something?" Miss Simperson insisted.

"Why, ma'am, it is something—something which does not belong to me. There, ma'am, I can say no more."

He did not have time to say more, whether willingly or unwillingly, for Mrs. Creevet now returned, with flashing eyes and uplifted nose, exclaiming—

"I have been robbed, I have been robbed; give me back my property immediately!"

"Who has robbed you?" inquired Miss Simperson, in astonishment, "and of what have you been robbed?"

"Who has robbed me—who is the thief? How can I tell? But of this I am confident, that somebody has been to the closet outside my bedroom door, and carried off a deportment apparatus—and what is worse, a ten-pound note which, by accident, I had left in the apparatus—ring the bell, if you please, Miss Simperson, and I will send to Crayford for a policeman."

Thompson during this speech was a study for a painter of the passions. His face was white as death; a cold sweat stood on his brow; his fingers trembled as, standing behind Miss Simperson, he furtively examined the unlucky apparatus, and found inside it—a ten-pound note! Poor man, I do not envy him his feelings!

"Stop," said Mrs. Creevet, "before I send for a policeman, I will examine every person in this room to begin with, and afterwards the maids and other servants. There has not been time as yet for my property to be carried off the premises."

"As you please, ma'am," said Miss Simperson, proudly; "but if you have been robbed, as you say, of a ten-pound note, I am sure you will not find it here. Now, my dears, let us form in a line—That is right—You, Thompson, can stand here, next to me."

Thompson, who had contrived to place his unwelcome burden on the table, among the school books, took up his position where Miss Simperson indicated. Everybody, except Mrs. Creevet, noticed his extraordinary paleness. As for Mrs. Creevet, she carefully searched each one of her nieces and their cousins—shaking their clothes, and turning out their pockets—all, of course, to no purpose. When she came to Miss

Simperson and Thompson, she contented herself with throwing
at them several suspicious and angry glances; but the governess,
laughing heartily at the absurdity of the proceeding, turned out
her pockets also, and instructed old Thompson to do the same.
Mrs. Creevet was forced to acknowledge the innocence of those
whom she ought never to have suspected, and left the room,
discontented with herself and everybody else, to pursue her
investigations in " the servants' hall."

As soon as the door was closed, the gardener precipitately
picked up the unlucky apparatus from the table, and thrust it
into the governess's hands, saying, in a broken voice, and with
great emotion—

" Give it back to her, ma'am, as soon as you can ; but oh,
don't say it was me !" Observing Miss Simperson's look of
surprise, he continued, " Yes, ma'am, I am the unfortunate
person who took the happaratus and the ten-pound note !"

Strong man as he was, even in his declining years, he
seemed quite overcome as he uttered these words; he felt
that if Mrs. Creevet became aware of the incident, he would be
placed in a very awkward predicament, from which the evidence
of the young ladies would hardly extricate him. So far as Miss
Simperson was concerned, his character was cleared at once by
Miss Bertha's acknowledgment that it was at her urgent request
and her sister's that Thompson had carried off the apparatus,
not perceiving, of course, the bank-note that Mrs. Creevet had
dropped upon it. In the circumstances the governess saw that
she must resort to a little stratagem. Taking the note and
apparatus, she undertook to put the latter in the kitchen fire,
and take on herself the responsibility ; as for the note, she
would pretend to search for it in the closet, and, it need hardly

be said, *would find it there*, and return it to the sorrowing proprietor.

Thompson, greatly relieved, went back to his duties in the garden, and the young ladies, sobered by the risk they had incurred of involving an innocent man in very serious trouble, sat down to prepare their lessons for the morrow.

II.

On the following afternoon a merry party was assembled in the drawing-room of Prospect House, for the four young ladies, Matilda and Florence, Bertha and Alice, assisted by Miss Simperson, were busily engaged in filling vases and china bowls with fresh-cut flowers in honour of the expected home-coming of Mrs. Morton and Mrs. Brandon. The girls were radiant with fun and laughter, in which their governess heartily shared, and the only shadow on the picture was the presence of Mrs. Creevet, who sat bolt upright in the most uncomfortable chair in the room, hemming a pocket-handkerchief, and sadly regretting the days of yore, when, in the presence of their elders, young people were taught to show a due respect by sitting still and silent. How unbecoming, how "unlady like," how indecorous, were those loud laughs and rapid movements of the body—jumping here, springing there, now kneeling on a chair, now standing on a cushion ! How could Miss Simperson countenance such very unrefined behaviour ! Well, for her part, she would not keep in her house for a week—no, not for a day !—a person so ill-fitted to train young ladies properly, so sadly ignorant of the very elements and principles of a wise system of education. Hum, ha ! And the fine Roman nose sniffed the air contemptuously. At last, as the merriment increased, she could possess her soul in patience no longer, and exclaimed—

"Bertha! Alice! be quiet, I command you! The noise is overbearing! One would think you were common children, just home from a Board School!"

Board Schools were Mrs. Creevet's pet aversion. She did not approve of educating "the lower orders."

"Oh, aunt, we haven't seen mamma for six weeks, and we are expecting her every minute! Isn't it jolly?"

"Jolly! What a dreadful word! But because your esteemed mother is coming home is that any reason why you should turn this room into—into—hum, ha!—a bear-garden."

"I think I hear the carriage," said Matilda, and all four girls rushed to the windows.

"No; a false alarm," said Bertha.

"This is intolerable," exclaimed Mrs. Creevet. "Bertha! Alice! come here, and sit by me, and do not move until I give you leave."

"Oh, aunt!" muttered Alice.

"Do you hear what I say?"

"But, aunt——"

"Let me have no *buts*, miss. In *my* childhood, when my mother—I was not so disrespectful as to call her *mamma*—when she was absent I waited her return in the drawing-room, with my book or some needlework to occupy my attention."

"But when you heard her coming?" interrupted Bertha.

"I stood in the middle of the room until she entered, and when the door opened——"

"You ran to her of course," said Alice, "and threw your arms round her neck?"

"No, indeed! I was too well brought up to be so forward. I waited until she came up to me, and then made a low curtsey while she bestowed a kiss on my forehead; nor did I dare to speak until she first spoke to me!"

"Oh, horrid!" exclaimed Bertha; "I could never——"

"Mamma, mamma! here she is!" cried Matilda; and in a moment the four girls were out on the landing-place, hanging over the banisters, talking and laughing, while Mrs. Creevet threw herself back in her chair, lamenting that in six whole weeks she had been unable to refine the rude manners of her nieces, and resolving to give them a final lesson in deportment. So that, when Mrs. Morton and Mrs. Brandon entered, with the children clinging to them, and advanced to embrace Mrs. Creevet, to their astonishment she received them with a profound inclination of the body, and drew back to allow them to pass.

"Why, my dear sister," said Mrs. Brandon, "such a cold reception?"

"Not at all," said Mrs. Creevet. "I wished only, before kissing my dear sister-in-law, to do honour to the mistress of the house."

"My dear sister, don't see in me the mistress of the house, I beg of you; and let me thank you at once for so kindly taking charge of the children in my absence."

"I deeply regret that my exertions have not been crowned with the success I could have desired."

"What? have you any cause of complaint against Bertha and Alice? I am surprised—as they are really very good children, and easily managed."

"Excuse me, if I do not reply to your question now. When

L

you have rested, I shall be glad of an opportunity of explaining to you my fears and my hopes."

Here, Mrs. Morton, who had listened with much amusement to the brief dialogue, thought it best to retire from the scene, with her two daughters. Mrs. Brandon, seating herself on a couch, observed that she would relieve Mrs. Creevet of a burden which seemed to have weighed heavily upon her.

" Let us defer, until a suitable occasion, all discussion on this important subject," said Mrs. Creevet, loftily. "I cannot treat it as lightly as you seem disposed to do."

" Excuse me, Sarah " (Mrs. Creevet's Christian name ; she was very proud of it, because it was Biblical), said Mrs. Brandon, "but your seriousness and coldness alarm me. Have Bertha and Alice really given you cause of complaint? "

"Not so much cause of complaint, as of pity and deep regret."

" Why, children, what have you been doing in my absence ? "

" Well, mamma," said Bertha, " I do not say we might not have behaved better, but it isn't possible to get along with Aunt Creevet, for she scolds—and scolds—and scolds all day long."

" Bertha, I am shocked ! I cannot allow you to speak in that way of your aunt ! "

"But, mamma," cried Alice, " it is really true! All day long, as Bertha says, she grunts at us—"

" Alice, hold your tongue ! " exclaimed Mrs. Brandon, "go and ask your aunt's pardon for speaking so disrespectfully."

"No, mamma, I had rather not," replied Alice, with a pout.

"What ? you would rather not ? Is that the way in which you answer me ? Alice, I fear you have forgotten yourself."

" Forgive me, mamma, I was wrong ! But when I have to

ask aunt's pardon, she makes me go down on my knees, fold my hands, kiss hers, and repeat such funny words that I forget them directly."

"You are talking like that, Alice, in order to excuse yourself. Obey me at once, and ask your aunt to overlook your impertinence."

With slow step Alice went up to her aunt, and saying—

"Pardon me, aunt, and I will not be so naughty again—" was about to kiss her, when the high Roman nose was loftily elevated, and drawing herself up to her full height, Mrs. Creevet drew back a step or two, and said—

"You must not expect to embrace, Miss Bertha, a person whom you have insulted! You must wait respectfully and modestly until she is willing to pardon you: then you must not throw yourself upon her with vulgar offensiveness, like an ill-bred milk-maid, but salute her deferentially, advance discreetly, and kiss the hand which she graciously extends to you. Hum, ha!"

She suited the action to the word; but Alice, taking no notice of the graciously extended hand, returned, weeping, to her mamma, who, vexed at Mrs. Creevet's want of judgment, caressed her daughter, and praised her for her obedience. She invited her to help in unpacking the presents which she had brought from Scarborough, and with Alice on one arm, and Bertha on the other, left the room.

"Deplorable! humiliating!" exclaimed Mrs. Creevet, "the mother is in as much need of rigid training as her daughters! You cannot fail to see, Miss Simperson, that she professes to be quite satisfied with Alice's pretended excuses."

"Oh, ma'am, it would be better," said Miss Simperson, "if

you would adopt the new ways. Educational systems are not so—so—perfect as they were in times past ! "

" The right word, Miss Simperson, the right word, and I thank you for it. Perfect ! Yes, the system under which *I* was brought up, might well be called "perfect." In my young days respect was esteemed the first of the sciences. And it *is* a science—a true, a grand, a beautiful science ! Now, all the talk is of love ; and *that* they call progress. But it is ridiculous, nay, impertinent to love those whom we ought rather to fear and respect. There are those, Miss Simperson, whom we ought to fear, those whom we should respect, and those whom we may love."

The governess, repressing a smile, hazarded the remark that it was possible both to respect and to love, and even to combine love and fear.

" No, ma'am," said Mrs. Creevet, solemnly, extending the forefinger of her right hand, and shaking it warningly. " We fear God and the Queen. We respect our parents, our superiors, our elders. We love our children, our equals, and our domestic pets."

She would probably have enlarged on this futile subject, had not Mrs. Brandon made her appearance. That amiable lady was a good deal distressed, because she had already recognized in her children a change for the worse ; such a change as she could hardly have thought possible in so short a time. " They have lost," she said, "their docility, their sweet tempers, their joyousness ; they were always on the most affectionate terms, but now they dispute with one another about trifles ; they answer me quite smartly, and delay in obeying my orders ; yes, they have changed, and not for the better."

"Yes, indeed, Mrs. Brandon," replied Aunt Creevet, "it is as you say, and the faults you speak of have been the object of my solicitude and of my stringent discipline. I would like to have handed them back to you as docile as machines, as calm and tranquil as sleeping waters, silent as statues, courageous as Leonidas and his Lacedemonians, polished as the ladies of the old *regime*. I have not succeeded. I required longer time and more absolute authority. In vain I resorted to severe remonstrance and corporal punishment ; they were neutralised by the knowledge that in a few weeks or even days my government would be at an end."

"Your remarks are a source of grief to me in two ways. I see that my poor girls have been unfortunate, and that you have taken a great deal of trouble without the satisfaction of success. Let me thank you cordially for your conscientious attention, and at the same time beg of you to excuse the shortcomings of my daughters towards you."

"It will give me much pleasure to continue and complete their education."

"No, Sarah, thank you ; the education of our daughters is a duty which Mr. Brandon and myself can never devolve upon others."

"As you please, Mrs. Brandon," replied Aunt Creevet, stiffly ; "be not afraid that I shall mix my ideas with yours ; they are as incompatible as oil and vinegar."

And she withdrew to console herself with reflections upon the superiority of the Old Ways as compared with the New.

"It is only too evident, Miss Simperson, that I made a mistake in entrusting my daughters to the care of their aunt. She does not understand the management of children at all.

But why have they never written to me? Or why did you not let me know how things were going on?"

"I did all I could to protect your daughters, but you had given Mrs. Creevet the most absolute control, and of course I supposed that you were acquainted with her educational methods, and approved of them."

"No, I had never seen my sister-in-law except as a visitor. I knew she bore a very high reputation, and when I went with Mrs. Morton to Scarborough gladly accepted her offered services in order to relieve you from a charge which, however, I knew you were quite willing to accept. But what is the meaning of this?"

She might well inquire, for in rushed her two daughters, pulling one another, and quarrelling at the top of their voices.

"I say that I will tell mamma," blurted out Alice.

"And I forbid you to tell her," said Bertha, angrily.

"If you think I shall pay the least attention to anything you may say——"

"If you don't listen to me, Alice, I'll tell mamma that you made Thompson steal."

"And if you dare to tell her that, I shall let her know that you stole grapes in the vinery."

"And I'll tell her that Alice speaks untruths."

"And I shall say that you are a thief also."

"Hold your tongue, you story-teller."

"Leave me alone, you thief."

"What do I hear? What dreadful words are these?" exclaimed Mrs. Brandon, re-entering the drawing-room. "I am not at all surprised now that your aunt complained of your bad manners. How long is it since you have learned to indulge in such gross language."

" Bertha is always wanting to tell tales of me," said Alice, " in order to get me punished, and I don't want to have the straps and backboard put on me again."

" And I don't want to be shut up in the Black Hole, and get whipped every five minutes until I ask pardon on my knees. Besides, when I report you I get a reward, and so I *shall* tell mamma that you have taken——"

" Hush ! I will not hear a word. Are you not ashamed, children, to be quarrelling like this within an hour of my return home ? And have you forgotten that I do not like tale-bearers, and never listen to their tales ? "

" But, mamma, Aunt Creevet ordered us to report each other," said Alice.

" And when we had nothing to report," said Bertha, " she punished us because, she said, we were hiding something from her."

" And why *did* you tell such shameful stories about me, Bertha, when you knew I had done nothing wrong ? "

" And why did you say that I had thrown my fable book into the pond ? "

" Silence, children, I command you ! " exclaimed Mrs. Brandon. " You little know the pain you are causing me by these revelations of misconduct."

" Oh, forgive me, mamma," cried Bertha, embracing her fondly ; " but why did you leave us so long with that cruel aunt ? "

" Yes, dear mamma," said Alice, " do not leave us with her again. She makes us naughty, very naughty, as you see for yourself."

" I can promise you that Aunt Creevet shall have charge of

you no more.. But why did you not let me know in your letters
what you are now telling me? You wrote to me on the contrary, that she was very kind and that you loved her dearly."

Bertha and Alice hung their heads.

"To tell you the truth, mamma," said Bertha, "she forbade
us to complain, and made us write our letters under her own
eyes. She always stamped them herself, and sent them to the
post. But we ought to have been brave, and have refused to
write what was not true."

"But why did you not ask your cousins to write?"

"Oh, mamma, she never left us alone with them; she said
they would corrupt our morals, because Mr. and Mrs. Morton
had indulged them so shamefully."

"And once I *did* write to Florence," said Alice, "on a bit of
paper, asking her to let you know how unhappy we were. But
she saw me slip the paper to Florence, got behind her, snatched
it from her, and read it. Then she dragged me upstairs and
whipped me until I cried; after which she shut me and Bertha
up in the Black Hole until dinner-time."

"The Black Hole? What do you mean?"

"It's a small, dark closet upstairs, mamma, on the attic floor.
There is no light in it, and its dreadfully hot, so we called it
the Black Hole—and oh, it's a horrid place!" cried Alice.

Mrs. Brandon clasped her two daughters in her arms, and
kissed them fondly. "All this that you tell me is very painful.
I am grieved to think my dear children should have suffered so
much."

Mrs. Morton, who had been discharging some pressing
household duties, now entered the room with her two daughters,
Matilda and Florence.

"Here we are, all assembled together once more—quite a happy family party. Papa will be home in a few minutes, and then we will go to dinner. But what has upset you, Margaret? You are looking pale and anxious."

"Bertha and Alice have been telling me of the harshness with which their aunt has treated them. I wish I had never asked your good husband to extend his hospitality towards her."

"Well," said Mrs. Morton," I have heard some almost incredible stories from Matilda and Florence. Aunt Creevet talks a good deal about the 'old ways,' of which she is such an admirer; but, as pointed out by her, they seem to bristle with thorns, and I much prefer the 'new.'"

"Their evil effects are very plain," remarked Miss Simperson. "The poor girls told untruths to avoid punishment, and rebelled against discipline because it was unwisely severe. Kept in a state of continual irritation, their tempers gave way, and they quarrelled with each other. But your presence and influence, ma'am, will soon restore order, and you will have no more reason to complain of Bertha and Alice than I have of Matilda and Florence."

Here the footman appeared to announce that Mr. Morton had returned, and that dinner was served. At the same time he handed a letter to Mrs. Morton.

As she took it from the salver she read the address.

"It is for you, Margaret dear," and she passed it on to her sister.

"From Aunt Creevet, I see," said Mrs. Brandon, opening it.

"Aunt Creevet? Is she ill? What is the matter?" inquired Mrs. Morton.

M

"Read it aloud, my dear," said Mrs. Brandon, handing it to her.

Mrs. Morton read as follows :—

"MY DEAR NIECE,

"You must allow me to release myself from a position which is at once *false* and *painful*. I am unable, without profound indignation, to observe the *vulgar manners* and *uncultivated deportment* of your two daughters, recently under my charge. I cannot be *silent*, and I am not allowed to *speak*. Unwilling to be harassed by the new ways of so-called *reformers*, whom I regard as *pernicious agitators* and *chimerical theorists*, and unable to make you understand the *superiority* of an educational system which the intelligent Miss Simperson justly characterised as *perfect*, I am compelled to inform you of my *irrevocable determination*. In two hours I leave Prospect House! I request you to convey to your sister and Mr. Morton my sense of the *amiable hospitality* they have shown me, and my *regret* that I am unable any longer to *enjoy* it.

"Believe me, my dear Niece, to be

"Your *affectionate* and *compassionate* Aunt,

"SARAH CREEVET.

"Prospect House, July 27th."

"It is unfortunate," remarked Mrs. Morton, "that she should leave us in so unkind a spirit, but I do not see how we can help it. Now let us to dinner; we must not keep papa waiting. I will let him read Aunt Creevet's letter to explain her absence ; though he will be sorry that any guest of his should, under such regretable circumstances, leave PROSPECT HOUSE."